REDISCOVERING
LIFE

REDISCOVERING

LIFE

Awaken to Reality

Anthony de Mello

IMAGE

New York

Published in the United States by Image Books, an imprint of the
Crown Publishing Group, a division of Random House, Inc.,
New York.
www.crownpublishing.com

IMAGE, the Image colophon, and Image Books are registered
trademarks of Random House, Inc.

Library of Congress Cataloging-in-Publication Data
De Mello, Anthony, 1931–1987.
    Rediscovering life : awaken to reality / by Anthony de Mello.—
1st ed.

        p. cm.
    1. Spiritual life—Christianity. I. Title.
    BV4501.3.D42 2012
    248.4'82—dc23

                                                        2011052078

ISBN 9780307984944
eISBN 9780307984951

Printed in the United States of America

Cover design by Laura Duffy
Cover photograph: Art Wolfe

10   9   8

First Edition

"Why have you hidden the secret of happiness from me?" the disciple asks the master.

"Did you hear that bird singing?"

"Yes," answers the disciple.

"Now," says the master, "you know that I have hidden nothing from you."

"Yes," says the disciple.

PREFACE

Very few times does a book come along that can really change your life. *Rediscovering Life* is one of those books.

Based on a satellite retreat that Tony gave in 1984 in coordination with Fordham University, *Rediscovering Life* once again brings his gift of storytelling—with messages of peace, acceptance, compassion, and enlightenment—to a contemporary audience.

Whether you're sixteen or sixty, it doesn't matter at what age you start reading Tony de Mello's wise words. It doesn't matter what page you start reading from or how many pages you read at a time. His words are abundant with wisdom—a wisdom that knows that growth takes place gradually or, on occasions, instantly. Sometimes, out of the blue, you wake up and everything is different.

Play with the words that follow in this book. Let them come into your mind at odd times—while standing at the checkout counter, while stuck in traffic, or while waiting to cross the street. Rediscover what it means to be happy and to experience abiding peace.

> Said the jilted lover, "I have burned my fingers once. I shall never fall in love again."
> Said the master, "You are like the cat, who having burned itself from sitting on a stove, refused to sit again."

The most expensive thing you spend in your life is your TIME!

Don't waste another second of it being unhappy!

> —Jonathan Galente and Desmond Towey,
> Trustees, De Mello Stroud
> Spirituality Center

REDISCOVERING
LIFE

Let me begin by telling you what I plan to do. The theme is the rediscovery of life.

I discovered something about ten years ago, and it turned my life upside down. It revolutionized my life. I became a new man. This is what I'm going to share with you. I am happy to share it with you, in a special kind of way, though you might say to me, "How come you heard this just ten years ago? Hadn't you read the Gospels?" Of course I'd read the Gospels, but I hadn't seen it. It was right there, but I hadn't seen it.

Later, having discovered it, I found it in all the major religious writings, and I was amazed. I mean, I was reading it, but I hadn't recognized it. I wished to God I'd found this when I was younger. Oh, what a difference it would have made.

So, how long will it take to give it to you? A whole day? I'll be honest with you: I don't think it will take more than two minutes. Grasping it or getting it might take you twenty years, fifteen years, ten years, ten minutes, or one day, three days—who knows. That depends on you.

Various people have told me over the years, since my initial discovery, that their lives were pretty much revolutionized, too. But not too many people—I'm sorry to say, very few have. I tend to think that if out of the one thousand people who are listening to me, if one person hears it, that's a pretty good average. Is it difficult to hear? Is it difficult to understand?

It's so simple that a seven-year-old child could understand it.

Isn't that amazing? And in fact, when I think of it today, I think, *Why didn't I see it?*

I don't know. I don't know why I didn't see it, but I didn't. Now, maybe one or another of you might see it today, or might see part of it. What would you need to see it? Just one thing: the ability to listen. That's all. Are you able to listen? If you can, you might get it.

Now, listening is not as easy as you might think it is. Why? Because we're always listening from fixed concepts, fixed positions, fixed prejudices. Listening does not mean swallowing, though. That's gullibility. "Oh, he says it, so I take it."

I don't want any of you to have any spirit of faith while you're listening to me. I mean, you could take what the Church teaches on faith; you could take the Bible on faith, etc. Don't take me on faith. What I want you to do is to question everything I'm saying, think about it, come back at me. Feel free to do that even while I'm talking. Ask questions, raise your hands anytime.

But then, listening doesn't mean attacking, either, though I'm going to say something that is so new that some of you are going to think I'm crazy, that I'm out of my mind. So, then, you're going to be tempted to attack. If you tell a Marxist there's something wrong with Marxism, the first thing he's likely to do is attack you. If you tell a capitalist there's something wrong with capitalism, he's up in arms. If you tell an American, "Hey, you know, there's something wrong with the United States"— and the same with the Indian person if you're attacking India, and so on.

It doesn't mean swallowing, it doesn't mean attacking. It doesn't mean agreeing.

Did you hear about the Jesuit superior who was a great success? People would ask him, "How come you're such a great success as a superior?"

He would reply, "Very simple. The formula is simple: I agree with everyone. I just agree with everyone."

They would say, "Don't be absurd. How can you be a successful superior, agreeing with everybody?"

He would reply, "That's right. How could I be a successful superior, agreeing with everybody?"

So, it doesn't mean agreeing with me. You could disagree with me and get it. Isn't that amazing? It means being alert. Be alert. Be watchful. Listen with a kind of a fresh mind. That's not easy, either—listening with a fresh mind, without prejudices, without fixed formulas.

Just yesterday somebody told me a story. You know the famous saying, "an apple a day keeps the doctor away"? Well, this guy was having an affair with the doctor's wife and was eating an apple a day, so—he got it all wrong. He got it all wrong! He was living from a fixed formula, see? A fixed position.

Someone also recently told me a story about a priest who was trying to convince an alcoholic parishioner that he ought to give up drinking. So, the priest gets a glass of alcohol, pure alcohol, and he gets hold of a bug, a worm, and he drops it into the glass. And the poor worm begins to wriggle and dies. And he says to the parishioner, "You got the message, John?"

John says, "Yeah, Father, I got the message. I got the message. You know, you got a bug in your stomach, alcohol is the thing to kill it." So he got the message, yes. John wasn't listening, see? He wasn't listening.

I know a case where a Father wasn't listening, either. This man goes to see the parish priest. The parish priest was reading the newspaper, didn't want to be disturbed. He said, "Excuse me, Father." Father was irritated; he ignored him. "Excuse me, Father."

Father said, "What is it?"

He said, "Could you tell me what causes arthritis, Father?"

Father was irritated. "What causes arthritis? Drinking causes arthritis, that's what causes arthritis. Going about with loose women causes arthritis, that's what causes arthritis. Gambling causes arthritis, that's what causes arthritis. Why do you ask?"

He said, "Because it says in the paper here that the Holy Father has arthritis."

Father wasn't listening, see? If you are ready to hear something new, simple, or unexpected against almost everything you've been told 'til now—ready to hear that?—then, maybe you'll hear what I have to say.

Maybe you'll get it.

When Jesus taught the good news, I think he

was attacked not only because what he taught was good but also because it was *new*. We hate anything new. I hated anything new. Give me the old stuff. We don't like the new. It's too disturbing. Too liberating. So, the ability to listen: Buddha formulated it beautifully. He said, "Monks and scholars must accept my words not out of respect, but must analyze them, the way a goldsmith analyzes gold: by cutting, scraping, rubbing, melting." You must not accept my words out of respect, but should analyze them by cutting—the way the goldsmith analyzes gold, see? Cutting, scraping, rubbing, melting. Okay, so we've got that clear.

What's this thing we call *life*? Take a look at the world and then I'll invite you to take a look at your own life. Take a look at the world. Poverty everywhere. I read in the *New York Times* recently that the bishops of the United States claim that there are thirty-three million people in the United States who are living below the poverty line, a distinction drawn by the government itself. If you think that is poverty, you ought to go to other countries and see the squalor, the dirt, the misery. You call that life?

Well, I've got news for you. I can show you life even there. About twelve years ago, I was introduced to a rickshaw puller in Calcutta. It's awful. I mean, a human being; riding in a rickshaw, you don't have a horse pulling you, you've got a human being pulling you. The life span of these poor men is from ten to twelve years once they begin pulling the rickshaw. They don't last very long. They get tuberculosis. They die quickly.

Now, Ramchandra—Ramchandra was his name—Ramchandra had TB. At that time, there was a small group of people engaging in an illegal activity involving exporting skeletons. The government eventually caught on to them. But you know what they used to do? They bought your skeleton while you were still alive. If you were very poor, you went to them and you sold your skeleton for the equivalent of about $10.

So, these people would ask the rickshaw pullers, "How long have you been working in the street?" Someone like Ramchandra would reply, "Ten years."

And these buyers would think: *He doesn't have much longer to live.* "All right, here's your money." Then, the moment one of these men died, they would pounce on the body, they would take it away, and then, when the body had decomposed through some process they have, they would take hold of the skeleton.

Ramchandra had sold his skeleton, that's how poor he was. He had a wife, he had kids, and he had the squalor, the poverty, the misery, the uncertainty. You'd never think to find happiness there, right? Yet, nothing seemed to faze him. He was all right. Nothing seemed to upset him. I said to him, "Aren't you upset?"

He said, "About what?"

"You know, your future, the future of the kids."

He said, "Well, I'm doing the best I can, but the rest is in the hands of God."

I said, "Hey, but what about your sickness? That causes suffering, doesn't it?"

He said, "A bit. We gotta take life as it comes." I never once saw him in a bad mood. But as I was talking to this guy, I suddenly realized I was in the presence of a mystic. I suddenly realized I was in the presence of *life*. It was right there. He was alive. I was dead.

Remember those lovely words of Jesus? Look at the birds of the air. Look at the flowers of the field. They don't sow, they don't spin. They don't have a moment of anxiety for the future. Not like you. He was right here. I know that rickshaw puller must be dead by now. I met him very briefly in Calcutta and then went on to where I live now, farther south in India. What happened to that guy, I don't know. But I know I'd met a mystic. Extraordinary person. He discovered life. He rediscovered it.

The human mind is such an extraordinary thing. It has invented the computer. It has split the atom. It has sent ships into space. It has not, however, solved the problem of human suffering, of anguish, loneliness, emptiness, despair. You're pretty young, most of you, but I honestly don't think you're strangers to loneliness, heartache, emptiness, depression, despair. How come we haven't found the answer to those?

We've made all kinds of technological advances. Has that raised the quality of our living by one inch? Want to know my opinion? No, not one inch. Oh, we have more comfort. More speed. Pleasures, entertainment—that's right. More erudition. Greater technological advances. What I'm saying is, has there been any improvement on ending that loneliness and emptiness and heartache? Any improvement on eliminating that greed and hatred and conflict? Less fighting? Less cruelty? If you want my opinion, I think it's worse.

And the tragedy is, as I discovered about ten

years ago, the secret has been found. But why don't we use it? We don't want it, that's why. Would you believe that? We don't want it. *We don't want it.* Can you imagine my saying to somebody, "Look, I'm going to give you a formula that will make you happy for the rest of your life. You'll enjoy every single minute of the rest of your life." Imagine my saying that to you.

Okay, I'm going to say that to you today. I'm going to give you that formula. You know what most of you are going to do? Sorry for insulting you in advance, okay? But if you're anything like the audiences I've had until now, you know what most of you are going to do? You'll say, "Stop it. Don't tell me. Stop it. I don't want to hear it." They don't want to hear it, and you don't even have to take that on faith; I'm going to prove it to you.

Falling into Happiness by Letting Go

Six months ago, I was in St. Louis, Missouri, giving a workshop. There was a priest there who came to see me. He said, "You know, I accept every single word you've said over these three days, every single word of it. And you know why? Not because I've done what you encouraged us to do—to cut and rub and scrape and analyze. No, about three months ago I assisted an AIDS victim on his death-bed. And the man told me the following. He said, 'Father, six months ago the doctor told me I had six months to live.'" The man was dying, see.

"'He said I had exactly six months to live, and I believed him. And you know something, Father? These have been the six happiest months of my whole misspent life. Happiest. In fact, I've never been happy till these six months. I discovered happiness.' He said, 'As soon as the doctor told me that, I dropped tension, pressure, anxiety, hope, and fell, not into despair, but into happiness at last.'" And the priest said, "You know, many is the time I've been reflecting on the words of that man. When I heard you this weekend, I thought, *The guy's come alive again.* You're saying exactly what he said." Here's a guy who had it. Here was a man who found it.

The formula's here; you've got it right here. It can be found in Philippians: "For whatever the situation I find myself in, I have learned to be self-sufficient. I am experienced in being brought low, and I have known what it meant to have abundance. I have learned how to cope with every circumstance: how to eat well or to go hungry; to be well provided for, or to do without."

That is, "I have learned to cope with every

circumstance: how to eat well or to go hungry; to be well provided for, or to do without." A little earlier, Paul says, "Rejoice always. Rejoice in the Lord. Again I say it: Rejoice." I think of Ramchandra in Calcutta. I think of that AIDS victim in St. Louis. That's what Paul is talking about. I had read it all my life and had never understood it. I mean, it was staring me in the face. I didn't grasp it.

Your Life Is in Your Hands

Okay, let's suppose *you want to grasp it*. Let's suppose *you want to see it*. What do you have to do? You have to understand a couple of truths about yourself.

What do you have to understand about yourself? First, your life is in a mess. Don't like to hear that? Maybe that proves that it's true. Your life is in a mess. People will say to me, "What do you mean, my life is in a mess? I'm doing pretty well in my studies, I got good parents, I got good relations with my family. I've got a boyfriend, I've got a girlfriend. Everybody likes me, I'm doing well at sports, and I have a pretty brilliant career ahead of me."

"Oh, yeah?"

"Yeah."

"You think your life is not in a mess? All right, tell me—here's the acid test. Ever feel lonely? Any heartache? Ever get upset by anything?"

"You mean—aren't we supposed to get upset?"

"You want the clean, clear, simple answer?"

"Yeah."

"No."

"You mean, not be upset by anything?"

"That's right, you heard me. No."

"Shut up. I don't want to hear any more."

See what I mean? He's got a theory, and it's that a person has to be upset or he's not human. Okay, go ahead and be upset. Good luck. Bye.

You know, there's a lovely saying, which I frequently quote. It says, "Don't teach a pig to sing. It wastes your time and irritates the pig." I had to learn that lesson the hard way. I've stopped trying to teach pigs to sing. You don't want to hear what I'm saying? Bye. No arguments. But I'm ready to explain, ready to clarify. Why try to argue? Not worth it.

So, ever suffer any interior conflict? No? All your relationships are going well with everybody? Yes? You mean, you're enjoying every single minute of your life? Well, not quite. . . . See what I told you?

Hey, wait a minute. The incarnation—yeah, yeah. All right, bye. See you later, alligator. Why argue? I'm not interested in arguing with you, period. I know because I was doing that all along. I'm not interested in arguing. You either face the fact that your life is in a mess or you don't. You don't want to face it, I've got nothing to say to you.

And now, "Your life is in a mess" means you're a victim of heartache, at least occasionally. You feel lonely. There's emptiness staring at you. You're scared.

"Me scared?"

"Yeah. Your life is in a mess."

"You mean, we're not supposed to be scared?"

"No, sir, or madam, as the case may be. No, you're not supposed to be scared."

"About anything?"

"About anything."

"But Mohammed was . . ."

"Excuse me, we'll deal with Mohammed later, all right? Let's talk about you."

Fearlessness. You don't know what it means. And the tragedy is, you don't think it's available. Yet, it's so easy to get. Since they told you it's not available, you never try to find it, but it's right here, all over the Bible, and you won't see it. Because they told you it's not available.

Are you anxious for the future? Any whiff of anxiety, worry, upset? Yeah, you're in a mess. How about that—want to clean it up? I'll clean it up for you in five minutes, depending on how ready you are. You don't have to move out of that chair. You can be sitting in that chair and you can clean it up in five minutes. And I mean that. This isn't a sales gimmick. I mean it. It's so simple and it's so deadly serious that people miss it. And you can have it.

Do you know how they discovered the diamond mines in South Africa? It's a very interesting story. I read it some time back. The author said that some guy, a white man, is there in South Africa, sitting at the hut of the head man of one of these South African villages. He sees the kids playing with what look like marbles. And his heart skips a beat when he recognizes that those weren't marbles at all; they were diamonds. He picks a couple of them up— they are diamonds.

So he says to the village head man, he says, "Could you give me some of these? You know, I've got children back home who play this sort of game too, and yours are a bit different. I'd be ready to give you a pouch of tobacco for this."

And the chief laughs. He says, "Look, this would be highway robbery. I mean, it'd be real robbery to take your tobacco for these things. We've got thousands of them here." So he gives him a basketful. The guy leaves, comes back with a lot of money, buys up all of that land, and within ten years he's the richest man in the world.

That could be a parable. It's tragic, it's painful. I think back on my own life and I think, *Why did I waste it?* I wasted it. And all kinds of wonderful things, believe me—pastoral ministries, theological enterprises, liturgical services, etc., etc., etc. The more occupied we are in the things of God, the more likely we priests are to forget what God is all about—and the more complacent we're likely to become. That's the story of Jesus. Who do you think got rid of Jesus? The priests—who else? The religious people. That's the terror of the Gospel, see?

So now, I think, *I wasted it*. But I don't have a minute's regret. Why waste even a minute regretting the past? But the fact is, I wasted it. I'm reminded of that powerful story of the fisherman who goes out early in the morning to fish, and it's too—whatever, I don't understand these things—but apparently it's too dark or something, and his foot hits upon something that seems like a sack. So he picks it up, probably washed ashore from some shipwreck or whatever. And he opens it and he can feel pebbles inside. So he takes these pebbles and he entertains himself until dawn, flinging those pebbles far out into the sea to see if he can judge from the "plop" how far he sent the pebble.

When day begins to dawn, he looks into the sack and he finds three precious stones there. God, the sack was filled with precious stones and he hadn't known it! Too late.

Not too late—three stones left. *Not too late.*

Let's go back and suppose that these people who were sitting on top of those diamond mines are starving. Their children are undernourished, and they're looking for food. They're begging, they're pleading with people to feed them. And someone says, "Hey, don't sell that property. You've got diamond mines. You see this thing? It's a diamond. You could sell it. You could get $100,000 for this, you. . . ."

They say, "That's no diamond. That's a stone." They got it in their heads that that's a stone. They refuse to listen.

Now, that's the condition of people everywhere. They don't hear you. They won't listen. You're telling them that life is extraordinary, life is delightful: "You could enjoy it. You wouldn't have a minute of tension, not one. No pressure. No anxiety. You want it?" The response: "Not possible. Never been done. Cannot be done." No spirit of research, of investigating, no "Let's find out. Let's go." No, no, no. Can't be done. "We don't want to hear you. I mean, our priests have told us it can't be done, our psychologists tell us it can't be done. You're coming to tell us it *can* be done?"

You Don't Want to Get Out of the Mess

So, the first thing: Admit that your life is in a mess. And, second—this is a bit tougher, okay? You ready? Here it is: *You don't want to get out of it. You do not want to get out of the mess.* Talk to any psychologist who's worth his name and he'll confirm that. The last thing a client wants is a cure. He doesn't want to get cured, he wants relief.

Eric Berne, one of your great psychiatrists here in the United States, put it very graphically. He suggested you imagine a client who's up to his nose in a cesspool, okay? Yeah, he calls it liquid excrement. And he's coming to the doctor, and you know what he's saying to him? He's asking the doctor, "Could you help me, so people won't make waves?"

The client doesn't want to get out of the cesspool. Oh, no, no, no. Get out? For heaven's sake, no. *Just help me so they won't make waves.* That's what he wants. He doesn't want to get out.

You want to test that on yourself? I'll give you a couple of minutes; you could do it right now.

Okay, here goes. Suppose you could be blissfully happy, but you're not going to get that college degree. Are you ready to barter your degree for happiness? You're not going to get that girlfriend of yours, or that boyfriend. Are you ready to barter them for happiness? Huh? How about this? You're not going to be a success, you're going to fail and everybody is going to call you a bum. But you'll be happy, you'll be blissfully happy. Are you ready to barter the good opinion of people for that? I'll give you time to think about it later.

When I was in Syracuse last summer, I saw something in the newspaper. It was an ad showing a girl holding onto a boy and she says, "I don't want to be happy. The only happy people I know are in a lunatic asylum. I want to be miserable with you."

See what I mean? "I don't want to be happy; I want to be miserable with you." She'll develop a theology about the damn thing after a while.

People don't want to get out of it. They don't want it. "I don't want happiness; I want fame." And, "I don't want happiness; I want to get that gold medal at the Olympics." Suppose I tell you, "Look, give up the gold medal, you'll be happy, damn it. What do you want that gold medal for? What do you want to be the top, the boss of the corporation for? I'll make you happy. On $10,000 a year, I'll make you happy."

"No, no, no, no, give me my money, my money, my money, my money, my money."

See what I mean now?

Now you're catching on. People don't want to be happy. They don't want to live. They want money. You know that guy, Ramchandra, the rickshaw puller? He lived like a king. I mean it. Foreign aid is fine; he didn't need foreign aid. Not to live. He needed foreign aid for comfort. He needed it for health. Not for life. He might have needed it for longevity, which means a long existence. You call that life?

See, Ramchandra was living. I was dead. He knew what life was. He was happy. He was like the birds of the air and the lilies of the field. He was an incarnation of the Sermon on the Mount. It was all there, in the Sermon on the Mount, I discovered later. It's all there. I hadn't seen it. Ramchandra lived like a king. What does it mean to live like a king? You know what idiots think it means? And the world is peopled with them, believe me. Idiots. You know what they think it means? It means moving around in limousines, having everybody curtsy to them and salute them, and all that sort of rubbish, all that sort of garbage—have their names in the headlines. They think that means having power over people. They think that's what it means to live like a king.

I'll tell you what I think it means. They're not living like kings, they're slaves. They're terrified. Look at their faces on television. For heaven's sake. Those kings and queens and presidents and the rest of them, look at them on television. You'll recognize it at once. He's scared. You know why he's scared? Because he wants power, that's why. He wants prestige. He wants a reputation. He's not living like a king.

You Can't Acquire Happiness— You Already Have It

I'll tell you what it means to live like a king: To know no anxiety at all. To have no inner conflict at all. No tensions, no pressures, no upset, no heartache.

So, then, what are you left with? Happiness, undiluted. People sometimes say, "What do I do to be happy?" You don't do anything to be happy, silly. It shows how bad your theological education has been if you think that you've got to do something to be happy. You don't have to do anything to be happy. You can't acquire happiness. You know why? Because you have it. You've got it right now. But the whole time you're blocking it with your stupidity. You're blocking it. Stop blocking it and you'll have it. If I could show you how to get rid of your conflicts, your anxieties, your tensions, your pressures, your emptiness, your loneliness, your despair, your depression, your heartache—if you could get rid of all that, what are you left with? Sheer, undiluted happiness, that's what you would have.

The Chinese put it beautifully: When the eye is unobstructed, they say, the result is sight. Don't do anything to get sight. When the eye is unobstructed, the result is sight. When the ear is unobstructed, the result is hearing. When the mouth is unobstructed, the result is taste. When the mind is unobstructed, the result is truth. And when the heart is unobstructed, the result is joy and love. You've got it all, but it's obstructed. Drop it.

So, second major step: Recognize that you don't want to get out of it. You want comfort. You want your little possessions. You want the little things that society has falsely taught you are essential for happiness. You want that. You don't want to get out of the mess. Those are the things that are creating the mess.

I'm going to give you something to think about. Has it ever occurred to you that what you call your happiness is really your chain? For example, are you calling *somebody* your happiness? As in, "You are my joy." It could be your marriage, your business, your degree, whatever. In whom do you find your happiness? Whatever the answer is, that's your prison. Oh, this is hard language. But reflect on these words—cut, scrape, melt.

You've Been Programmed with Wrong Ideas

Here's the third thing: Your life is in a mess because you have wrong ideas. It's not because there's anything wrong with you. You're okay, and I'm okay. You're okay, we're all okay. We're great. There's nothing wrong with us. But, they put wrong ideas into our heads. Somebody did. We needn't spend too much time trying to catch the culprit. But anyway, you have wrong ideas.

You know, if somebody has given you a stereo

set, then you received a manual of instructions along with it. Well, they didn't give us a manual of instructions when they gave us the gift of life. Or, let's put it the other way. They gave us the manual of instructions, but it was all wrong. So you're not getting music, you're getting scratchy sounds. You're getting upset, you're getting conflict, you're getting loneliness, you're getting emptiness. Oh, it is right there in the Bible, but very few people read it, really. They think they do, but they miss the point. I missed the point. Maybe I'm an unusually big idiot, but I discovered lots of company after a while. They missed the point, too. They didn't get it.

Desire Is the Root of Unhappiness

All right, so what is the point?

Now, there are many ways of putting forth the formula. I'm going to give you the simplest I've found. I'm going to give it to you in the words of old Buddha. Why did I choose him? Because his words are the simplest of all. But you find the formula everywhere. It's proclaimed with limpid clarity. You're probably going to disagree with it, but you can't miss the point.

Here it is: The world is full of sorrow. The root of sorrow is desire. The uprooting of sorrow is desirelessness. Oh, I'm imagining your faces. It's wonderful. You're thinking, *That's great, that's great*, but then you're thinking, *Wrong. That's awful!* Ha, ha, ha; isn't it wonderful? Because I know how I used to react to this. The world is full of sorrow, great. Right. Agreed. The root of sorrow is desire. Well—all right. Now, what are you going to conclude? The uprooting of sorrow is desirelessness. So I'm going to be a vegetable? I mean, how do we live without desires?

Let me give you a better translation. I don't think Buddha would be so foolish and stupid as to say that we ought to have *no* desires. For heaven's sake. I wouldn't be speaking if I didn't have the desire to speak. You wouldn't be here if you didn't have the desire to come and hear me. So let's give it a better translation.

The world is full of sorrow. The root of sorrow is attachment. The uprooting of sorrow means the uprooting, the dropping of attachments. You know, there are desires on whose fulfillment my happiness does *not* depend. In fact, you've got lots of desires on whose fulfillment your happiness does not depend. Or else you'd be climbing walls; you'd be nervous wrecks. We, all of us, have two types of desires. We've got some desires—we desire all kinds of things, and gee, we're happy to get them, and when we don't get them, it's okay, too bad. We're not unhappy. But we've got other desires—good Lord, if we don't get them, we're going to be miserable. That's what I mean by an attachment.

Where do you think all conflicts come from? Attachments. Where do you think greed comes from? Attachments. Where do you think loneliness comes from? Attachments. Where do you think emptiness comes from? You got it, same cause. Where do you think fears come from? Attachments. No attachment, no fear. Ever thought of that? No attachment, no fear.

"We'll take your life."

"Go right ahead. No attachment to life. Happy to live, happy to let go."

Do you think that's possible? Well, you want to know something? People have attained it, so it is possible. Want to attain it yourself? Ahh, attachment. "Sorry, sir, you have AIDS. You only have six months to live."

"Just six months? Boy, that's a lot of time to live—that's wonderful." Happiness. Hey, this guy's got no attachments.

Here's another example. You walk into a restaurant. You think you'll have soup tonight. "What
kind of soup do you have? Do you have tomato
soup?"

"No, sorry, sir, no tomato soup."

"No tomato soup? For heaven's sake, I mean,
what kind of a restaurant is this? Come on, folks,
we're going somewhere else." See, if you don't get
tomato soup, you can't have dinner. Attachment.
Here's what happens when there's no attachment:

"What kind of soup do you have, tomato soup?"

"No tomato soup."

"Well, what do you have?"

"We've got sweet corn, we've got mushroom
soup, we've got chicken broth, we've got . . ."

"Pretty good, I like all of those. How about
mushroom?"

I'm going to cheat on old Buddha right now and
slip another little example in while we're on this
point. You know, when you enjoy the scent of a
thousand flowers, you're not going to feel too bad
about the absence of one flower. Nobody ever told
you that in your culture, did they? They didn't tell
me, either. But when you enjoy the taste of a thousand dishes, you're not going to feel too bad about
the absence of one dish. Do you recollect being

educated to enjoy a thousand dishes, so that nothing upsets you? See, we missed it.

That's what your culture and mine are training us for. We got the wrong instruction. They don't give a damn whether you and I are happy or not. They want us to achieve. They want us to produce. That's what *they* want—even if we're going to be miserable slaves and unhappy. "So, big deal. You lost a friend. You got one . . ."

"No, not that kind; I want one personal, unique, unsubstitutable friend. So if he rejects me, then I'm miserable for the rest of my life."

Good luck. Bye. I'm not teaching this pig to sing. Too dangerous.

But that's the way we've been brought up. That's the way it has been for thousands of years. We've got to have desires on whose fulfillment *our* happiness depends. That's very good for so-called progress, of course, huh? Because you'll throw all you have into the enterprise. So-called progress. I call it "so-called" because that's not progress to me. That isn't progress.

"You mean, isn't it progress when we have jumbo jets and spaceships?"

Very clever. I'll tell you what progress is: Heart progress. Love progress. Happiness progress. "You got that?"

"Oh, sorry, we don't have that."

You can keep the rest—what's the use of it? Tell me, what's the use of moving around in an airplane with a heart that is full of misery and emptiness? Tell me. I'd rather live on the ground in a jungle and be blissfully happy and dancing all day. Wouldn't you? Maybe you wouldn't. I don't know.

Attachment Is the Enemy of Love

You see, you're really confronting a choice between life and death, and what people call life is frequently death, though they don't know it. And you mean to tell me that if you've got attachments, you can love? The biggest enemy of love is attachments. Desire, in the sense of attachment. You know why? Because if I desire you, I want to possess you. I can't leave you free. I've got to get you. I've got to manipulate you so that I can get you, if I desire you in this way. I'm going to manipulate myself, so that I can hoodwink you into allowing me to get you. Are you following what I'm saying? Clear enough? There's no fear in perfect love. You know why? Because there's no desire.

Now, ask your culture; I've asked mine. Ask your culture if it can make any sense out of this statement: Where there is love, there is no desire. That's desire in the sense of attachment, okay? You know what they will tell you? "But attachment is love." That's how stupid they are. Expecting to find life here? You can find only death and misery.

Such a simple, such a sublime, such an extraordinary thing. I run into people of all kinds, religious and nonreligious people, people who are atheists or whatever, and Catholics or lay people, priests and sisters and bishops. And I rarely run into someone who knows what love is. They all got the wrong instructions.

Attachment means, "I gotta get you." It means, "Without you, I will not be happy. If I don't get you, I won't be happy. I cannot be happy without you." There, you've got the formula for divorce. There, you've got the formula for quarrels. There, you've got the formula for friendships falling apart. "I cannot be happy without you. I need you for my happiness. By damn, I'll do everything to manipulate you, to get you."

Love means, "I'm perfectly happy without you, darling, it's all right." It means, "And I wish you good, and I leave you free. And when I get you, I'm delighted; and when I don't, I'm not miserable." Well, what do you know? I have learned to be self-sufficient. I'm standing up on my own two feet, not leaning on you. And you know, if I get money, that's wonderful; and if I don't get money, I'm not depressed. I'm happy. You know something else? When you go away, I don't—maybe it's too soon to say this here, but anyway, I'll risk it—I don't miss you. I don't feel pain. Where there is sorrow, there is no love. Tell me, when you grieve, whom are you grieving for? Whose loss? That's self-pity.

Oh, don't call it that. You're telling the truth now.

Here's the Formula

Here's a secret formula for you. If you were not actively engaged in making yourself miserable, you would be happy. You see, we were born happy. All life is shot through with happiness. Oh, there's pain; of course, there's pain. Who told you that you can't be happy without pain? Come and meet a friend of mine who's dying of cancer. She's happy in pain.

So, we were born happy. We lost it. We were born with the gift of life. We lost it. We've got to rediscover it. Why did we lose it? Because we were working actively. They taught us to work actively, to make ourselves miserable. How did they do that?

By teaching us to become attached. By teaching us to have desires so intense that we would refuse to be happy unless they were fulfilled.

The tragedy is that all you need to do is to sit down for two minutes and just watch how untrue that assumption is—that you would be unhappy without *A* or *B* or *X* or *Y*, or whatever. Do you know something? You won't sit. Because if you sit, you might see it. You won't sit and look at it. I know I wouldn't. I resisted it for years.

"You mean, if I don't get Mary Jane, or I don't get John, I won't be happy? Hey, wait a minute. Come to think of it, you're right. Before I met her, or him, I was happy. You know something? I once fell in love with somebody and then, well, I lost her, and I was heartbroken. And what happened? I'm all right now. So she wasn't my happiness, after all." Remember the time that you were a child and you lost something, and you thought, "I'll never be happy without this . . ." What happened? If we gave it to you today, you wouldn't even look at it.

False Beliefs and Illusions

Why don't we learn? Because we've got to live in illusions. It feels good. It gives us a kick, doesn't it? It certainly gives me a kick. We want kicks; we don't want happiness. We want thrills. And wherever you've got a thrill, you've got an anxiety, because you might lose that thrill, or you may not get it. And then you've got depression following that, you've got a hangover.

It's so simple. As I told you, I could put it down for you in two minutes. Whether you'll hear it, though, is another matter. That depends on your own heart. So here it is: The world is full of sorrow. The root of sorrow is attachment/desire. The uprooting of sorrow is the dropping of attachment. How does one drop attachment? You only look and see that it is based on a false belief—the belief that, without this, I cannot be happy. That's false.

The moment you see that belief is false, you're free. Good luck to you. It may take you one minute, it may take you twenty-five years. But the day you see it, you're free. You're free as a bird. You'll be coming up to give retreats, you'll be talking to presidents. You'll be meeting popes. You won't be fazed one bit. You're free. You're completely free.

You'll be making an ass of yourself, and it won't bother you. You won't bother to impress anybody.

You know what it means when you don't give a damn—is *damn* a swear word in the United States? Maybe I shouldn't be using it. You don't give a tinker's damn what they think about you and what they say about you. You know what that means? Oh, boy, that's freedom. You're not bothered about whether they approve of you or they don't. It's all right. You're happy. You don't approve? All right, too bad; you move on. You're happy. But that's because you've discovered that your happiness does not lie in these things. You've got to see that for yourself. It's useless reading a book, useless listening to me. You've got to *see* it. And, of course, you won't see it if you've got the wrong formula, get it? So I gave you the right one.

All right, let's take some questions:

> ~ *Does the dropping of attachments translate into detachment from the material world? Also, we've been taught to identify with the sufferings of Christ. Can we do that if we're always happy?*

Does the dropping of attachments mean detachment from the material world? No. One uses the material world, one enjoys the material world, but one doesn't make one's happiness depend on the material world. What I'm saying is, you really begin to enjoy things when you're unattached because attachment brings anxiety. If you're anxious when you're holding on to something, you can hardly enjoy it. So, what I'm offering you is not a withdrawal from enjoyment; it's a withdrawal from possessiveness, from anxiety, from tension, from depression at the loss of something.

The second question was a pretty good one, too. We're taught to identify with the sufferings of Christ. How would this link up with what I was saying about happiness? Let me clarify this a bit. Maybe the best way to do it is by means of a story.

Attitude Is the Difference

There was a great Zen master who was reported to have attained enlightenment. One day his disciples said to him, "Master, what did you get from enlightenment?" And he said, "Well, I'll tell you this: Before I was enlightened, I used to be depressed. After I got enlightened, I continued to be depressed."

Puzzling, huh? You see, the depression didn't change; his attitude toward the depression changed. He's not saying, "I'm not going to be happy until this depression goes away." Because, strange as it may seem, you could even be serene and calm and happy while the depression is going on. You're not fighting it, you're not upset about it, you're not irritated about it. You're serene. That's the difference.

~ *If happiness is not attachment, how do you define happiness in positive terms?*

Wonderful! Happiness cannot be defined. At least, I haven't found a definition. As a matter of fact, you have no idea of what happiness is until you've dropped attachment, so it could only be defined as the dropping of illusion, the dropping of attachment. When misery caused by attachment is dropped, happiness is attained.

Of course, one could use words like *peace, serenity, being above it all, enjoying every moment as it occurs, living in the present.* They're words. You don't know what sight is until the eye is unobstructed. You don't know what happiness is until attachment desires are dropped. Then you know. And the words don't matter anymore.

~ *If Christ is a model for us of detachment and of happiness, how do we identify with His loneliness in the garden and His anger in the temple and being forsaken on the cross?*

Christ Himself went through periods, it would seem, of loneliness, of anger, of abandonment on the cross, etc. Are these states compatible with happiness? What do you think? Is it possible that either because of one's programming, because of one's culture, or simply because of one's human psyche and body, one would go through all kinds of sufferings and yet somehow be above them all? What do you think? Yes? No? What?

Before enlightenment, I used to be lonely. After enlightenment, I'm still lonely, but loneliness isn't what it used to be anymore. We Christians continually teach that Jesus was a man. He was a human being like everyone else, and like every human being, He was subjected to all of these things. Does one eventually outgrow them? Some of us do, and others don't. Jesus could outgrow them, and may not have outgrown them. One knows so little about this. But this much is clear—that one does have a state of serenity, of happiness, even when these clouds pass by. By way of example, consider this:

You've got the clouds and you've got the sky. Many of the Oriental masters will say that enlightenment, before they *saw*, meant they would identify themselves with the clouds. After enlightenment, they would identify themselves with the sky.

> ∼ *You've been saying a lot about being able to experience suffering and depression and yet still be detached from it. I'm trying to understand clearly what you're saying, but it seems such a contradiction to say that you can be happy and depressed, since depression, as I've always been taught, is the absence of contentment and happiness. Could you explain this a little more?*

That's a good question. Aren't depression and happiness two contradictory states? I think this is what you're asking, right? Yes and no. If for you happiness means thrills, fun, pleasure, then, yes, they are contradictory. But thrills, fun, and pleasure are not happiness. What are they? They're thrills, they're fun, they're pleasure. They're not happiness. Happiness is a state of nonattachment.

For many years, I didn't even think such a thing existed. For me, to be happy meant to have fun. To be happy meant to win, to get what I wanted. This is what people ordinarily understand by "happiness." Most cultures understand happiness to mean that when you get what you want, you're happy. You know the way it is: "Yea, I got what I wanted, I'm happy." But that isn't happiness. That's the thrill. That's getting what you want.

Depression is frequently—though not always—not getting what you want. It's the opposite of the thrill. If you're going for thrills, you're going to be depressed. It's the other end of the pendulum swing. Oh, you're going to have to do a lot of thinking on that. It's the thrills that cause the depression. Of course, depressions have physical causes, too. So you see, I'm not talking about happiness as meaning thrills, fun, pleasure. I'm talking about happiness meaning that one is above it all. One is serene. One is not attached to its coming and going.

There's one more thing I'll add: The more you fight depression, the worse it gets. Don't resist evil. When they strike you on one cheek, turn and offer the other. When you take away one devil, seven more come. You deal with these things by not fighting them. Because the more you fight them, the more you empower them.

Challenges of the Catholic Church

~ The nature of my question is quite different
from the previous ones. Assuming that I am
attached to my experience as a religious Catholic,
U.S. woman, and that I have been educated in
the post–Vatican II time; and second, assuming
that I am also tempered by my experience of the
total change and transition that that has meant
in the last twenty years, I'd like you to apply your
beginning metaphor of the monks and scholars
being challenged to analyze words the way
goldsmiths analyze gold, cutting and scraping
and rubbing and melting. I'd like you to apply
that metaphor, if possible, to the current situation
in the U.S. Church.

Let me say this quite unambiguously: I think that
the Church in the United States, in quite a number
of areas, is at the cutting edge today. It's offering
leadership to the rest of the world, and particularly
in the matter of women's rights. And I think that
centuries hence, the Church is going to be grateful
for this.

And, of course, you're running into difficulties.
Every time change is in the offing, you're going to

run into conflict because people hate change. They don't want change. They want progress without change. So, you're naturally feeling the birth pangs and teething difficulties in the Church, but let me add this. You know, there's a lovely section in the Hindu scriptures, the Bhagavad Gita, where the Lord Krishna speaks with Arjuna, sort of the main character in the book. As some of you may probably know, the scene is of a battlefield, and the young prince is saying, "Why do I have to get into battle?" And the Lord says to him, very beautifully, "Plunge into the heat of battle and keep your heart at the lotus feet of the Lord."

That's the formula. Plunge into the heat of battle and keep your heart at the lotus feet of the Lord. At peace. Is it possible to go into the din of battle, to fight the good fight, and be at peace? Of course, it is. All the great mystics attained that. Because if you're not at peace, believe me, you're going to do much more damage than good. You know why? Because it isn't the Lord's battle you're fighting, it's the ego's battle.

~ *When you talked of true freedom, you said not to bother whether someone approves or disapproves. If they don't approve, you say, "So*

*what, I'm happy." I have a difficult time with
that because it sounds sort of selfish. I thought
you should also have freedom in doing things for
others, not necessarily for approval but just for the
sake of giving.*

Maybe I didn't make myself clear enough. I'm not saying that we don't care about other people. We care very much. We're very sensitive to them. But we're not controlled by their approval or disapproval.

So, you're very sensitive to people, and you're giving them what you think is good for them, but you're not being controlled by them. In other words, I'm not going to desist from what I think is good just because you disapprove; and I'm not going to do what I think is bad because I think you approve. So, I'm not being controlled by you. Only then can there be true love.

The Mystical Quality of Religion

*∼ Why does religion often get in the way of
happiness for people?*

I wouldn't say that religion always gets in the way of people. It's always in danger of losing its mystical quality, though. You want to see politics? You find it in religion. You want to see dirty infighting? You find it in religion. You want to see crucifixion of a messiah? Where do you think you get it from? Religion.

It's a sad irony, and it's right there in the New Testament. The horror of the New Testament is that it was reserved for the religious people to crucify the messiah. Not the Romans, not the colonialists, not the multinationals, not the imperialists, not the bloodsuckers or the moneylenders, but the religion. That's the horror of the New Testament.

So, it is true that religion is always in danger of doing this. But religion also preserves the mystical element. I think we'd be too one-sided if we denied that. You know, heavens, would I have seen what I have seen all these years if I had not been a Jesuit? Yes, the organization has lots of disadvantages, tremendous disadvantages; I can see that.

I sometimes think it's something like how we see our moms. Moms have their good points and their bad points. Yet we love our moms in spite of it all. Sometimes we don't take too much notice of what she's saying. She belongs to another age, and sometimes we take some of her great wisdom and we learn to assess what's good and bad, and we love her just the way she is. So, I can see how it is important for us to always be on the alert, we religious people, to see that religion doesn't come in the way of the truth and of the mystical, and that it also, thank God, still keeps some of its beauty and some of its original goodness.

Detachment from Hoping, Dreaming, Grieving?

~ *First, does "no attachment" mean that we should not participate in the very human, creative endeavors of hoping and dreaming? Second, how do you suggest that we deal with feelings of loss and grief and the other things that are part of our human experience?*

All right. Does it mean that we withdraw from the human endeavor, having no attachment? No. Plunge into the din of battle. And you know, you have so much more energy, believe me, when you have no attachments. You've got all of your energy available to you.

The great Chinese sage Tranxu puts it marvelously: "When the archer shoots for nothing, he has all his skill. When he shoots for a brass buckle, he is already nervous. When he shoots for a prize of gold, he goes blind. He's out of his mind. He sees two targets. His skill has not changed. But the prize divides him. He cares. He thinks more of winning than of shooting. And the need to win drains him of power." Isn't that sublime? The need to win drains us of power. If we don't need to win, we have so much more energy.

So, no one joins in the human enterprise of human dreams and visions and goals so marvelously and so creatively as the person who is unattached. Unfortunately, we've come to associate nonattachment with not caring, with not enjoying, with asceticism. No, I'm not talking about that at all. You'll see this as we go on.

And that second question is a bit more touchy. Well, shall I tell the truth or shall I soften it? What do you think? You better decide that. Soften it? All right, we'll say it like it is. I wouldn't grieve if I weren't attached. I wouldn't grieve if it were not for my loss. I wouldn't grieve if, in some way, you were not my happiness. But when I enjoy you wholly, I love you in the sense of, "I'm sensitive, I care. It is your good I see."

And I leave you free. And you are not my happiness. I have not given over to you the power to decide whether I will be happy or not. Then, I do not grieve at your absence or at your rejection. Or at your death. That's hard. You may need many months to digest that one. But grief is wonderful. You drain it out of your system gradually and then you come back to life again.

How to Clean Up the Mess

~ *I think that a lot of people believe that the world is in a mess, but they don't think that their own lives are in a mess, and they want to solve the world's mess through commitment to causes. So, how do you distinguish between commitment and attachment, or commitment and detachment?*

There are two things there. First, the world is in a mess, I'm in a mess. Don't hide behind a peace committee; it solves nothing. When a bunch of wolves sit in on a peace committee, you're not going to get peace. When a thousand wolves organize for justice, you're not going to get justice. You've got to deal with the world. So, he's so right in saying, we've got to take a look at ourselves, too.

But then there's the other thing: How does one

commit oneself to a cause? That's fine. Commit yourself wholeheartedly to the din of battle—but be above it. As somebody said so beautifully once, "For peace of heart, resign as general manager of the universe." I'm not the general manager; I do what I can. I plunge in, and the result is left to God, to life, to destiny.

Detachment and Success

~ *There seems to exist a tension between being aware of a state of detachment and also [sensing] that pull toward what society says you have to do to be successful. How do you resolve that tension, or even that sense of one's pride that gets in the way when you become aware of that [tension]?*

It's like a pull. On the one hand, there's happiness, peace, serenity, being—self-possession, being above it. On the other hand, there's the drive that society has put into us to be successful. How does one resolve it? Just redefine success. What is success?

Now, that's not going to come easy if you're too much in the grips of what others will think, what others will say. I wouldn't call it pride. I'd call it a kind of total dependence for one's worth on others. *If you think I'm worthwhile, I'm worthwhile. If you adjudge me a success, I'm a success. If you don't I'm not.* Oh, who will give us the grace to break out of that?

When I meet a man or a woman who has broken out of that, I salute. Not the other ones, the big commanders and the presidents. Very inferior human beings. Not one bit better than the average. Lustful, greedy, frightened, anxious, ambitious, grasping, controlled like puppets by what people think and what people say; and so captured, so enslaved by the desire for power and—listen, you want me to respect that?

But then I run into a guy like Ramchandra. He has my admiration. I run into the kind of person— for example, that AIDS victim in St. Louis. I didn't have the privilege of meeting that man, but that man has my admiration. See, we're admiring the wrong things, and this goes for most of our religious institutions. They say: "You gotta make it." And they're so honored that an ex-alumnus has become *x, y,* and *z.* Is this what we value? Or do we value the person who has broken out of the clutches of society? Do we value riches? Like, you're giving a million dollars, you get the front row. We're brainwashed, we're bombarded constantly by this viewpoint. We're indoctrinated.

Three Stories That Speak to the Mystical of Things

There's a Japanese master, a fellow called Bokoju. See, every time I think of his name, I imagine a plump, rotund kind of a guy, happy-go-lucky soul, Bokoju. It was said of Bojoku that every morning when he woke up, he'd give a great big belly laugh that resounded through the 250 cells of the monastery. Everyone could hear him. Everybody woke up with that laughter, like the alarm clock, see? Great big belly laugh. And he'd go on for about three or four minutes. And the last thing he did at night before he went to bed was, again, to let out a great big belly laugh, and then he'd curl up on his mat and go to sleep.

And the disciples were very curious to know what it was that made the master laugh. And they tried their very best to get him to tell them. But he wouldn't. And he died without telling them. That's the end of the story. So, all kinds of people have been trying to figure out what it was that made him laugh. I've got a couple of hunches myself.

We have an Indian mystic called Kabir. Kabir has some extraordinary mystical poems, and one of them begins with the line, "I laughed when they told me that the fish in the water is thirsty." How about that one? "I laughed when they told me that the fish in the water is thirsty." You mean, he's in the water? Mm-hmm. There are fish? Mm-hmm. You're thirsty? Oh, come on. But we are, aren't we?

Or another line that I read last summer by an American who was hunting in Africa. He said he lived with some natives there, and whenever they were in danger, he said it was quite extraordinary. "They'd look at us white men with a strange kind of curiosity when they saw fear in our eyes. It was incomprehensible to them"—to this particular group of natives, okay? "It was incomprehensible to them," says this writer, "like looking into the eyes of fishes who were afraid to get drowned." That's pretty good, too. Can you imagine a fish scared of drowning?

And so again and again, the mystical teachers of the world have been posing this question. They're puzzled. "Why are they unhappy?" That kind of thing. "Why are they scared?" That kind of thing. And, of course, until one has *seen*, it makes sense to feel scared. It makes sense to be unhappy.

Unreal Fear

When I talk about fear, I'm not talking about a present response to immediate danger—that, the animals have. I'm talking about fear of what's going to come, fear of what's going to happen. I'm talking about that. And this, the mystics tell us, doesn't exist in their mind. Simply doesn't exist. Boy, what a state to be in. Extraordinary.

Well, here we are with these. There's another nice story about this, about a camel trader, who's walking across the Sahara Desert. The party pitches a tent for the night. And the slaves drive pegs into the ground and tie the camels to the pegs. Then they come in to say to the master, "There are only nineteen pegs and we've got twenty camels. How do we tie the twentieth camel?"

And the master said, "These camels are stupid animals. Just go through the motions of tying the camel and he'll stay put all night," which is what they did, and the camel stood there, convincing everybody. And next morning when they lifted the tent and continued on their journey, the slaves came to complain that all the camels were following except this one. This one refused to budge. And the master said, "You forgot to untie him."

They said, "Oh, yes," so they went through the motions of untying him.

That is an image of the human condition. We're scared about things that are not. We're tied to things that don't exist. They're illusions. They're falsehoods. They're beliefs; they're not realities. The agonies we go through over things that we have—we have convinced ourselves that our happiness depends upon them, but it doesn't. We don't want to see it. Again, the mystics understand this because they went through these things themselves. They're amazed that human beings would deceive themselves in this way.

The Beginning of Freedom

Now, what I'm going to offer you today is the beginning. You don't need anyone else to show you the way. If you keep following this, if you just get a glimpse of this and you keep at it, you'll find the way; and sooner or later, you'll discover what this means. You're tied to things that don't exist. They don't exist.

There is a story about a disciple who goes to the master and the master says, "What have you come here for?"

And the man says, "Moksha." *Moksha* is the Sanskrit word for "freedom." "I've come for freedom."

"Oh, freedom," says the master. "Mm-hmm. Go and find out who has bound you."

So the guy goes back and meditates for a week, and he comes back and says, "No one has bound me."

"Then, what do you want freedom for?" says the master. And in that minute, the disciple's eyes are open and he attains freedom. He attains liberation.

What have you come here for? Freedom. Go and find out who has bound you. Well, no one has bound you. Then, what do you want freedom for? You're free already. Why do you seek it? You don't understand it because you've tied yourself with all kinds of imaginary chains.

I think it was John Lennon who said, "Life is something that happens to us while we're engaged in something else." Oh, beautiful. Beautiful. Life is something that happens to us while we're busily engaged in something else. Worse: Life is something that happens to us while we're busy suffering all sorts of other things.

Life Happens

And I have a perfect image for this. Think of a concert hall. The orchestra is to play a symphony. You've settled down nice and comfortable in your seat and you're ready to hear the music and to enjoy it, and then suddenly you remember that you forgot to lock your car. Oh, gosh, what do you do now? You can't get out—it'll be too disturbing. You cannot enjoy the music, and you're caught in between. That is the image of life for most people. Constant anxiety. What do I do now? What's going to happen next? How do I cope with this? How do I deal with that?

You mean, *Is another condition possible?* It is, it is. It is. You know, what are you religious for? What is the use of your religion if it isn't giving you this answer? You got the dogmas right, you got the beliefs right. You got the ritual right, you got everything right—but your life is all wrong. What's the use of it? You got the menu, but you got no food to eat. You got all the "Lord, Lord" right. But there's no life, huh? *Why do you call me Lord, Lord, and not do what I'm telling you?* What's the use of it if you don't know how to use it? So here goes. How does one use it?

Let's begin with your being upset. What is it that upset you? Somebody died? Somebody betrayed you? Someone rejected you? You lost something? Your plans have gone awry? Something's gone astray? Whatever. Can you think right now even as I'm talking of something that has upset you in the recent past? Go on, do it. I'm going to give you three or four seconds to do that. Think of something that has upset you in the recent past or is upsetting you right now.

Nothing in This World Upsets You

Get your soul ready for a shock. Here it comes. I say it just like it is; I'm going to lob the bomb right into your midst. Listen to this: Nothing in reality, nothing in life, nothing in the world, upsets you. Nothing has the power to upset you. Did anyone tell you that? All upset exists in you, not in reality. You can underline the word *all*. All of it. All of it. All of it. All upset is in you, not in life. Not in reality. Not in the world. It's in you.

Just understanding this has changed the lives of people, I mean, 180 degrees. Just understanding this, and no more. Reality is not upsetting. Reality is not problematic. If there were no human mind, there would be no problems. All problems exist in the human mind. All problems are created by the mind. Somebody said to me in Denver last summer, "Wouldn't there be some problems that exist in reality and not in me?" I said to him, "If we take you out of there, where's the problem?" No problem.

Now, to me, this is a truth so simple a seven-year-old child could understand it. But I've met people who are doctors and all sorts of other things, and they never understood it. Never understood it. They just took it for granted that problems exist in the world. Problems exist—by "problem," I mean something that upsets you, okay? I'll repeat that. By problem, I mean something that upsets you. People think that the problem exists in the world. They think that it exists in other people. They think that it is in life. No, no, no. It's in them. As simple as that. Nothing has the power to upset you.

It's Your Programming That Causes the Upset

Now, let's work this out concretely. Somebody broke a promise, okay? You're upset. What do you think upset you? Broken promise? Hmm-mm. I could bring another individual here in your place who is also faced with a broken promise but is not upset. How come you got upset? Now, you were trained to think that it was the broken promise that upset you. But it wasn't the broken promise: It was your programming. It was your training. You've been trained to upset yourself every time you're faced with a broken promise.

You're planning a picnic on Sunday and the picnic gets rained out. Where do you think the upset is—in the rain or in you? In the rain—or in your reaction to the rain? The upset feeling is not caused by the rain, but by your reaction to the rain. Someone else would react differently: no upset. If you had not made your happiness depend on its not raining, you wouldn't react this way, right? But you and I have been trained to make our happiness depend on certain things, and so when those things don't happen, thanks to our training, thanks to our programming, thanks to that false belief *If this doesn't happen, I'm not going to be happy*, well, what do you know? We upset ourselves.

There are some very interesting examples of this; let me give you examples from other cultures. Last summer, a friend of mine here in New York gave me a little anthropological detail of a tribe in Africa. He said, "Their method of awarding the death penalty is the following: They don't have any electric chair, they don't have death by hanging. They have death by banishment. So, you belong to the tribe and if you have committed a capital offense, you're banished."

And this friend of mine said, "When the sentence of banishment is read, within a week or so, the person dies." Would you die if somebody read a sentence of banishment on you? I wouldn't. I don't think you would, either, would you? What do you think? I mean, we might feel terrible if we were banished to another place. But we wouldn't die, for heaven's sake. They die. Literally.

False Belief Leads to Death

A Jesuit friend of mine in Mexico told me about the belief among the natives in one part of Mexico that if they touch a certain type of stone, they will die. They're quite convinced of this. So, there was a youngster who was running and his foot touched this kind of cursed stone; and the boy came to Father and said he was going to die. And Father said, "Oh, that's superstition. I don't believe this."

That night the boy's mother came to the priest and said, "Father, would you please come with the last sacraments."

And Father said, "Look, that's superstition. Don't you encourage that kid or he's going to really die—it's going to be a self-fulfilling prophecy. This is rubbish." Father didn't go. The next morning the kid died. He had literally died. He was convinced he was going to die, and he died.

One hears of students in certain cultures, in certain communities, in certain countries, who take their examinations so seriously that if they fail, they commit suicide. I know people who fail and say, "Great. Doesn't matter at all." But for somebody else, it's suicide. Why the difference in reaction?

Who killed that person? The examination? The failure? What do you think? What would you say? His reaction, right? Think of the guy who was banished from that African tribe. Suppose I said to the judge, "The banishment killed him." But the banishment did not kill him. It was his belief in its power, his culture, his indoctrination, his programming that killed him.

The kid whose foot touched the stone—did the stone kill him? Oh, no, no. It was his belief that it would, his programming. Now, let's apply this to daily life. When we do the application, it's devastating. It's explosive. You could explode into happiness forever—you really could. I'm going to get you to try, to give you a little bit of a break. I'll give you an exercise for this, and some of you are going to experience that happiness right now. Something has upset you. Did you hear that expression? *Something* has upset you. That's the way the English language is. That's the way all languages are. "Something upset me." Nothing upset you. The accurate way to speak would be, "I upset myself on the occasion of something." But who speaks like that? You say, "You upset me." No. "Your behavior caused me to get upset." We hate that, don't we? We love to make the world responsible, or people responsible, or life responsible, or God responsible: "You did it." Not the upset.

Spirituality Means Not Being at the Mercy of People or Events

Are you getting some inkling of what it would mean if you really grasped this? You'd be above it all. That's one nice definition of spirituality. Spirituality means no longer being at the mercy of an event, or a person, or anything else. I didn't say not to love people. I said, You're not at their mercy anymore. You're no longer at the mercy of an event, or of a person, or of anything else. In other words, no matter what happens, you no longer upset yourself.

We spend years studying spirituality, writing about it, reading books on the subject, taking courses on it—but are you still upset? Do you still upset yourself on occasion? You do? What's the use of all your studies? Life is passing you by while you're sitting in that concert hall, unable to enjoy the music, unable to lock the car, caught in between.

Now, let's see if we can work this out concretely. Think of two or three examples of upsetting situations or upsetting persons. If the example is personal to you, that would be even better, but it doesn't have to be personal. It can be something that you've experienced or something that someone else has experienced.

What if someone dies? What upset you? The death of this person? No. If you're upset by it, you've been programmed to be upset when someone dies. Now, take your time with that. That goes against everything your culture and mine has taught us. We've been taught to upset ourselves when we lose somebody. We've been trained to upset ourselves when someone rejects us, disapproves of us, leaves us, dies on us. We've been—here it goes, get ready for a scandalous sentence—we've been trained to depend emotionally on people. To not be able to live emotionally without people. I stress "emotionally."

So, naturally I'm upset because someone I was attached to has died. The death has upset me. On the occasion of this, I have been trained to upset myself. It sounds almost blasphemous, huh? It's awful. Think it over.

Here's another example. You see someone on the street who doesn't have enough to eat. It seems like we ought to be upset. Is that an evil? What do you think? Yes or no? Yes, obviously. Ought I do something about it inasmuch as I can? Yes or no? Yes. Good, great. So far you're getting all the right answers, but I'm going to catch you—watch out.

Do I need to upset myself in order to swing into action and do something about it? You know, there's an assumption that if you don't upset yourself, if you don't train people to upset themselves, they're not going to do anything. But look: Here's someone who doesn't have enough to eat, and that's a calamity. Now, you've gone and upset yourself. We've got two calamities. Could we deal with this calamity without having another one added?

Plunge into the Din of Battle

But you know, lots of people cannot even conceive of swinging into action without their first upsetting themselves. It's something like this: You're standing in a line. Somebody breaks into the line. Now you want to take action. That's fine. You want to say it's wrong. You're right. You want to do something about it. You want to push them away. That's fine. But you know what you're doing? You're saying, "You've misbehaved, so I'm going to punish myself."

Look at what you are doing. He misbehaved, right? So, what you're going to do is raise your blood pressure, lose your peace of mind, miss your sleep tonight. Say, "Look, since you misbehaved, I'm going to . . . ." Why would you punish yourself? You're innocent. But you'd think people would understand this. I mean, educated people, so-called reasonable people. Their culture is built on this. How could you not upset yourself? You mean, you're not upset? No. But you're planning to do something, evidently. Oh, yeah, very much so. But you're not upset? No, why should I upset myself? Why should I punish myself because he misbehaved?

Plunge into the din of battle and keep your heart at

peace at the lotus feet of the Lord. But there's a fear, see. The people who trained us, the people who programmed us, feared that if we didn't upset ourselves, we wouldn't do anything. It never occurred to them that when you upset yourself, you have less energy to do something and you have less perception. You're not seeing things right anymore. You're overreacting.

Don't Waste Your Breath

I know nothing about boxing, but they tell me that the last thing a boxer in the ring ought to do is get upset or lose his temper, because then he's lost the match. They tell me, too, that the first thing his opponent is trying to do is to get him to lose his temper, so that he loses coordination and perception. And how often do people who get into social projects—great projects, for the welfare of others—get so involved emotionally and so upset that they destroy the very work they set out to do? They lose perception. They overreact.

Now, suppose there's a crime done against you. Shouldn't you be upset about that? For example, someone has stolen something from you. That's a crime done against you. Does that justify upsetting yourself? Yes or no? No. But it seems almost unrealistic to even think in these terms. Now, do you understand what I mean when I said that people don't want to *hear*? They say, "Oh, get away, you're crazy, you're mad. Get away."

Does this remind you of the Gospels? "We don't want to hear you. Go away, go somewhere else." Don't waste your breath. They don't want to hear. They don't want to be happy. They don't want to change. All right, let them be. Why would you want to waste your breath? Do you have a need to give yourself the good feeling that you're converting everybody, that you're the cause of their enlightenment? Maybe you ought to look into yourself now. You're not going to be happy unless you set yourself up as the great master, huh? See? They don't want to hear? Great, all right. That's their problem.

Nothing in this entire world has the power to upset you. Nothing. As a matter of fact, nothing has ever upset you. Nobody has ever hurt you. You stupidly hurt yourself.

Now, that brings me to part two. Oh, they didn't hurt me, right? Reality didn't hurt me, right? So I cannot lash out against them. So, who did the damage? Oh, me. Me hurt me? Yeah. And I'm going to lash out against me. I'm going to hate me for doing this. Are you getting what I'm saying? Why do I do this? I'm getting angry with me. I'm getting upset with me.

Well, I got good news for you. They didn't do it to you. The world didn't do it to you. Life didn't do it to you. And best of all, you didn't do it to you. Isn't that wonderful? Then, who did it? Look, honest-to-goodness, would any of you in your right mind sit down and knowingly and willingly and deliberately upset yourself? Come on. Do you think any of you would do that? No, we wouldn't. We're not going to upset ourselves deliberately. It's as if this is something beyond our control, right? So, stop blaming yourself.

This has been stamped into you. You've been programmed with this. You've been conditioned this way. But this is what you've got to understand. You see, you don't have to do anything for enlightenment. You don't have to do anything for liberation and for spirituality. All you have to do is see something, understand something. If you would understand it, you would be free.

Maturity Is Blaming No One

So, "I'm upset. I've upset myself. They did it to me."
Wrong. "I did it to me." Wrong. It's your programming that's doing it to you. It's the culture that's
doing it to you. This is the way you've been brought
up; this is the way you've been trained. That native
in Africa is banished, and the sentence killed him.
Wrong. He killed himself. Wrong. It was his programming that did it.

You know, one of the signs of maturity is the
following. It's very hard to define maturity, but I've
come up with a fairly workable definition: Maturity is when you no longer blame anyone. You
don't blame others, you don't blame yourself. You
see what's wrong, and you set about remedying it.
That's one pretty good sign of maturity.

You know, you'd be amazed how childish people
are. They're so childish. I mean, have you seen a
little child? As a matter of fact, you can almost take
for granted that, in its present state of lunacy, 99.999
percent of humanity is childish. Just hang around.
Hang around for half a day; you'll find our greatest
men and women indulging in acts of childishness,
utterly childish.

You know the way a child behaves? I don't know

about here in the States, but in India, they bump their knee into a table and say, "Waaah." Then everybody goes, "Who hit you, the table? Naughty table. Naughty table." And so, "Oh, oh, oh, table, naughty table." And then the kid feels good. See how childish that is? So now they're coming to you and they ask, "Now, who hit you?"

"My wife, my husband, my superior."

"Aren't they awful? They're terrible." And the little baby is feeling good. And he's the president of a big association, or country, or whatever.

My God, how childish can people get? And they don't know their childishness. They've got to blame somebody. But, no. Maturity is understanding that no one is to blame. Or better still, and more accurately put, maturity is not giving yourself the childish emotional outlet of blaming others or yourself but, rather, seeing what went wrong and setting about remedying it. Doing something about it. See? So, they're not to blame. It's the programming that's doing this to you.

I know I'm repeating myself, but it's important. I'm going to offer you an exercise. It will only take a couple of minutes. See if it has any effect on you.

Think of something that until now you would

have said has upset you. I asked you to think about it a little while ago; go back to that thought. And understand that it wasn't that thing or that person that upset you. It was your programming. It wasn't their meanness, it wasn't their disapproval, it wasn't their rejection, it wasn't their failure. It was your programming that upset you. And see what happens to you.

When you're able to do this repeatedly, again and again, the general universal experience is the following:

First step: "Gee, this thing upset me."

Second step: "Huh-uh, it wasn't this thing that upset me; it was my programming that upset me. So, I don't have to deploy all of my energies fighting that outside thing, right?" Right. "I don't have to spend all my emotional energies blaming that outside thing." That's right.

Funny how this thing gets depleted. It keeps going down. Because as long as I've got an enemy out there who's upsetting me, I'm demanding that my enemy change. I'm refusing to give up my upset unless that thing has changed. Am I clear enough? If I think someone is upsetting me, then as long as he's there and he's indulging in the behavior that I say is upsetting, I'm refusing to give up my upset unless he reforms, he changes, he disappears, he gets away or whatever.

But let's suppose life persists in being in a certain way so you continue to be upset. Now, the moment you say, "Hey, wait a minute. It's not life, it's my programming," then someone could be right here, doing something, and you needn't be upset.

You Don't Have to Fix It

Now, for a while, you're getting less and less upset about fewer and fewer things. Now comes the big—pardon me, I don't mean to be insulting or anything, but you're going to enjoy this—now comes the big American question: How do we fix it?

"He's not upsetting me. I'm not upsetting me. The programming is upsetting me." How do you fix this? You know the big Oriental answer? You don't fix it. You let it be. It will go away. The more you try to fix it, the stronger it gets.

Gee, that's another mind-blowing thing: Don't fix it. Let it be. Let it be. It will go away. It really will. But don't we need to know where this programming comes from? It helps to know, but it's not necessary.

And if you're hell-bent on getting it—"I've got

to find out where it comes from and I've got to change it"—you're going to make it worse. You can be sure of that. Lots of people never change because they're so determined to change. They're so determined that they never change. They're so tense, they're so anxious, that it gets worse.

So here's another thing: We're all the same. You know, the kind of stuff I give you here, I give in Japan and I give in India, and I give in Spain and Latin America, and everywhere else. And everywhere, people are the same. You've got a thin veneer of culture that's different, but deep down we're all the same. The same problems are everywhere. The hatred is the same. The conflict is the same. The guilt is the same. The dependence on people's opinions and the emotional dependence on approval are the same. It's exactly the same. Just scrape off the exterior culture, we're all the same.

Now, everywhere, people are trying to fix "it," too. How do I change it? You don't change it; you understand it. You look at it, you observe it. It will take care of itself. Then what happens is that you don't change it; life changes it. Nature changes it. The way you don't heal yourself, nature heals itself. You just do something to aid nature.

When something happens that we commonly

say upsets us, it isn't this thing that upsets us. Life is not rough on us. Life is easy. It's our programming that is rough on us. Life is easy. Life is delightful. Think of my friend Ramchandra, the rickshaw puller. So it isn't this thing outside that's causing the upset. It isn't you that are causing the upset. It's your programming.

The Difficulties Are in Your Programming

You've got people you're living with, and you're having difficulty in human relations? Human relations are never difficult; it's your programming that's difficult. There are never any difficulties in relating to people. There are only difficulties in your programming. How come you're getting upset? You ask, "It's possible to live with a guy who's losing his temper every day and not get upset?" Yes. Yes, very much so, to not be upset. You ask, "When somebody insults you, you're not getting upset? That's right. "Why not? Why not be upset when someone insults you?"

I mean, when the letter isn't received, it's sent back to the person who wrote it. You don't receive it, it goes back. You know why you got insulted or why you were upset by the insult? Because you took it, that's why. Silly, why did you take it? "You mean that it's possible not to take it? You mean, you call this being human—living like a little monkey? Anyone pulls a little string and you jump?"

I'll tell you what it means to be human. You know what it means to be human? It's something like this: A guy buys a newspaper every day from a newspaper vendor. The newspaper vendor is always rude to him. So a friend of his says, "Why do you buy your paper from this guy? He's always rude to you. Why don't you buy it from someone else just next door?"

Says this guy, "Why should the vendor decide where I buy my newspaper? Why should he have the power to decide that?" Now, you're talking about a human being. Otherwise, you're talking about monkeys. You could control them; just twist their tail a little and they act in predictable ways. Programming. Programming.

So, it isn't the person who has upset you. It isn't you who have upset yourself. It's your programming. All you have to do is understand this and distance yourself from it, understand it. You want to do something about that programming? If you can, fine. Is it necessary? No. If you're understanding it, you know that it comes from your programming, not from you, not from them. It'll take care of itself, it really will.

You'll be amazed that, after a few months, things that before would have made you sick with anxiety, or with suffering, or with whatever, you can take in your stride with perfect peace. You're quite relaxed about it. That's the spiritual life. That's dying to yourself—dropping that programming. You drop it by understanding it for what it is. Call it by its name.

> ~ In the world you describe, is it possible to sin?
> Do we liberate ourselves, or does Christ's grace
> free us? May I not take action, even though I
> am not upset, at an injustice I see? If somebody
> jumps in line ahead of me, I'm not going to let
> them upset me, but may I take action?

We'll begin backwards. First, when somebody jumps into the line ahead of you, may you take action? Go right ahead and take action. Take all the action you want. Yes, it's okay. The point is, you're taking action to right a wrong; you're not taking action to relieve an upset feeling. You see the difference? That's a big difference. I'm sorry to say, frequently we take action not only to right something that is wrong but also to relieve upset feelings. That's bad.

Second, is it possible to sin in this world that we're talking about? Of course. There's so much sin around us. There's so much evil around us. However, the more you understand human nature, the less inclined you feel to judge anyone. Because there's so much stupidity, so much ignorance, so much fear, and so much programming behind so much of what we call sin, we've been rightly advised to judge no one. No one, not even ourselves. Paul says that; even he doesn't dare to judge himself.

And third, is it we who liberate ourselves or is it Christ's grace? Christ's grace is available to everybody. But you know, having Christ's grace available to you doesn't necessarily mean that you're going to get anywhere. You've got to do something. You remember the story of that guy who lit his pipe and burnt his beard, and they said, "You burnt your beard." He said, "I know, but can't you see, I'm praying for rain?" Well, yes; I mean, the rain is available, but you'd better pay attention to what you're doing.

So, the idea is, unfortunately, that God's grace is available to everyone. The tragedy of the human race is not that there is a shortage of God's grace;

it's that there's a shortage of proper understanding. We got wrong ideas that need to be corrected.

> ~ *Father de Mello, you have a great deal of education and travel in your background, and while these are not necessary for the enlightenment as you define it, I wonder if you could comment on how they prepare you as steps of growth to be ready to accept the truth that you speak of.*

Does an educational background prepare you for this sort of thing? No. You need common sense and intelligence, which has nothing to do with erudition, literacy, or learning of any sort. Period. Don't you go away with the thought that a PhD is better equipped than a simple, illiterate peasant in the Andes. Not for this. You'd be amazed at how little intelligence learned people have. You really would.

Yesterday a friend of mine at Fordham University was telling me that he read an extraordinary book about the people who sent some of these spaceships, these rockets, up to the moon. He said, "You know, it's tragic that we were able to produce all of this cooperation to send a rocket onto the moon, but we can't cooperate with our families.

We don't know how to do it. We don't know how to get on with our wives and husbands." See what I mean? I've run into peasants who know how to do that—cooperate. How about that? That is intelligence. So learning isn't the same as intelligence at all. You could have a lot of learning and no awareness of yourself at all. You could know how spaceships function and you wouldn't know how you, yourself, function. Education is no great help. For this, what is needed is not an educational background, but wisdom, understanding, and intelligence, which are acquired by cutting, scraping, melting, questioning, doubting. If you never question, if you never doubt what they taught you, you never doubt what your culture gave you, how will you understand all of this?

~ *What is your concept of happiness and what is it to be human to God? Also, I'd like you to clarify something on detachment for us. First of all, you said that our desire is what chains us. What about our desire for God? And is God to be found in desirelessness? And moreover, could we equate God with desirelessness? Lastly, what about the person who is being physically abused in a home? How can he detach himself from that?*

We'll begin with your last question, which is more difficult. Obviously, a person who is being physically attacked at home is going to find it much more difficult not to be upset than someone who contemplates the world from his window. Look, I'm not saying this is easy. I'm saying it's possible. And I'm saying that if you think it's impossible, you're never going to get there. Is it possible that people could be tortured and also be at peace? Yes. I've seen instances of this.

I read an extraordinary letter written by a prisoner in Nazi Germany who was tortured every day, and he knew he was going to be executed. The most sublime and lovely letters that he wrote to his family; I read those letters. I said, "How would this be possible?" I read these letters about twenty years ago. I know now that it is possible. But let's make a beginning. A journey of a thousand miles begins with the first step.

Let's deal with the guy who breaks into the line. Let's deal with the woman who's always nagging you, or with the man who's always insulting you. Let's begin there. And as I said, they're not causing the upset; the upset is coming from your programming.

I'm not saying that this means not identifying a

wrong when you see a wrong. I'm not saying that this means you're not going to take action; you are. But you're seeing where the upset is coming from.

~ *Does true happiness come from within our humanly desire and control for happiness, or does it come from a soul's desire to know God and to know Jesus Christ?*

The desire for God: St. Thomas Aquinas says in the introduction to his great *Summa Theologica*, "About God, we can say this much with certainty: That we do not know what He is." God is beyond the knowing mind, which is why we call him *Mystery*.

How does one desire what one cannot and may not even conceive of? What one speaks of in symbolical, analogical terms? So you see, when we talk about desiring God, we don't talk of God as an object out there, as a person out there, who we can fully conceive or understand, and so that doesn't fall into what I'm talking about. Because you know not what you're desiring.

So, frequently when people talk about desiring God, they will set up some kind of an image and begin to desire that image. But to desire the unknown, the unknowable, that which is beyond all human conception and understanding, the Mystery—what does that mean? We have no idea. Could we equate that with desirelessness? Maybe, maybe not.

But for heaven's sake, don't get distracted by this now. Get on with the task. We could have all kinds of theological discussions about the other thing, but in the meantime, get on with the task. Get on with self-observation, self-awareness, self-understanding, self-liberation. Then you will understand better, beyond understanding what God is.

> ~ How can we obtain maturity if we blame the programming? Isn't that being immature, because we're putting the blame on the programming? Doesn't that lead to saying things like, "The devil made me do that," or "I'm a victim of society"? In other words, evading the responsibility?

Do you *blame* your programming? No, you don't blame your programming; you understand it. Now, it's like saying, "You blame the devil"—poor devil, I mean, we're blaming the devil. Take responsibility. But one must take responsibility wisely, okay? Remember how I said the upset is not in reality, it's in you; remember that? Don't keep blaming reality—it's in you. But shall you blame yourself?

It's not mature to blame yourself when you're not to blame; you're not doing it deliberately. This comes from your programming. So that's what I mean. You're not blaming your programming, you're understanding it. That's where it comes from.

When you bump your knee into a table, you must understand that the pain is not in the table. The pain is caused by something that's happening in your knee. Something's happening in your knee, and that causes the pain. The pain is not in the table. Now, when you bump into reality, there's a pain caused within you. That pain is not caused by reality, but by something that's happening inside of you. You're not producing that pain deliberately. Who would deliberately want to cause pain for themselves?

Now, you have to understand what that something is. Why is it that with some people, this process doesn't go on, or they've released themselves from it, whereas with others, it does? This is responsibility—to understand. And as a result of understanding, to be freed from it.

~ *Concerning victims of violent crime, I feel that painful emotions and a lot of confusion and*

isolation are brought about by a situation like
this. And by having the idea that you mustn't
be upset in a situation like this, I feel it's a very
uncompassionate view toward people. I'd like
to know how you would be able to deal with
someone who is not at your level, and how would
be the best way to approach a person like this and
show an empathetic view.

When someone comes to you and is all upset—let's
say she is a victim of crime, or someone's mother
has died and he is full of grief. Now, you don't take
the attitude of, "Oh, you're grieving, you're upset,
there's something wrong with you"—oh, no, no,
no. You understand. Look, this poor person, even
if the grief comes from an attachment, if the pain
or the isolation comes from an attack, this poor
person isn't causing it. Have you understood that?
Have you understood me to say that? The person
isn't causing the pain.

We could sympathize with the person, we could
understand the person. We can be compassionate
with the person. And gently, when the person is
ready, explain where it's coming from. Because, ul-
timately, we're not being compassionate if we don't
give people the secret someday. Am I clear enough

there? For example, you've come to me and you're very upset because someone has injured you. I'll understand you. I'll understand where you're coming from, I'll be compassionate toward you. But someday, sometime, somewhere, if you're ready, I'll slip you the secret. That to me would be true compassion. You don't have to be this way. There's another way.

~ You say that it's not the people around us who have upset us, that it's not ourselves but it's our programming. Is it not the people who were around us who have programmed us when we were young?

They have. But they didn't set out with any malice to do this to us. They're the victims of what other people have done to them.

Again and again, people come to me who are so upset about their parents. They can't forgive their parents, they hate their parents. All right, I understand. I'm not saying that your parents did right or they did wrong. Maybe they did wrong. But look, could you understand them? Because that's what love is all about, see. Love is not blaming others. Love is not judging others. Love is not condemning others. Love is understanding. Can you understand where they came from? Can you understand how there's so little malice there, and so much ignorance? And so much goodwill, and so much helplessness, and so much programming, and so much confusion, and so much fear. Have you ever paused to understand this? Oh, then you'll understand what it means to love. That will change you, too.

~ *I understand now that my happiness consists of being free of attachments and desires. I understand that Jesus Himself could experience fears and hurts and anger, but still not lose that lotus place with the Father. But my problem now is, I also believe that my happiness does not live in a very passive human existence where I would become an unfeeling zombie. But I feel that somehow in the middle is a passion and an enthusiasm and a zeal that Jesus Himself had, without its becoming an attachment. So I'd like you to say something about passion and enthusiasm and zeal when it's not an attachment.*

Remember what I said about the archer? When there is no tension and there is no upset, all of the forces within you are unleashed. And now you will understand what true joy is. Now you will understand what true enthusiasm is. Now you will understand what it means to plunge into life with heart and soul—with what we call passion. Get right into it, surely, because you're no longer stabbing yourself with these programmed emotions.

> ∽ *I have a problem going along with the idea that we've been programmed to be upset. It would seem to me, by looking at very young children who haven't been programmed yet with anything, that they're naturally upset.*

You have a point here. You see, little children become upset when they don't get something that they think is vital to them and that is necessary for their happiness. Then, after a while they forget all about it or they grow up and they don't care for it.

A little child couldn't care less about people. You don't tell a little child that when somebody laughs at a person, it's terrible. You could laugh at a child—ha, ha, ha—and the child laughs back. You see, it's a drug. The control. When you're two years old, if they teach you that when they clap you're supposed to feel good; and when they say, "Arrrgh," you're supposed to feel bad, and you swallow that, you're finished. The programming has begun.

> ~ *What about in a case of a prisoner of war or someone who's got AIDS or a terminal disease? There's really nothing that you can do for them, but you still feel upset for them. How are you supposed to get around not feeling upset about this person?*

Take the case of the person who was told he had AIDS and only had six months to live, and he was perfectly serene. Now, you wouldn't want to be upset when he is serene, right? And then, let's suppose there's someone who's not serene, but who's upset. I'd say, gee, if you contemplated life and you know it's coming to an end, and it has to come to an end, if instead of reading so many books you spend more time looking out the window, say, at this gorgeous thing you have here in the States of the different seasons, and you see those leaves falling and changing color, think how much that tells you about life. When you've understood that, and you understand the flow of life. Well, he's upset; you're not going to help him by being upset yourself. Does it make sense?

*~ How would what you're saying apply to the
way we cause others deliberately to suffer?*

Do we ever deliberately cause someone to suffer?
Now, I'm going to try to say this as succinctly as
possible. It would probably require an hour, so I
hope I don't get misunderstood. But all the same,
I'm going to take the risk and say it.

When you do damage to someone, you know
that the first person you're damaging is yourself.
Does this make sense? When you nurture hatred
for someone, the one you're damaging first is yourself, right? Now, who does this sort of thing? Crazy
people. Who buys a brand-new watch for $3,000
and puts sand in it? Crazy people. Who sits down
to a meal and puts powdered glass in the meal to
destroy themselves? Crazy people. Crazy people
commit sins. They're out of their minds. They're
killing themselves.

*~ First, would you comment on someone
who seems to have a kind of behavior that just
completely controls them? Second, could you
relate that to how Paul says that he does things
that he doesn't want to do, and the things that he
really does want to do, he can't do?*

Let's deal with the first question. Some people seem to have achieved complete control of themselves through hardening themselves—not allowing themselves to feel. Do you see the difference between this and what I've been saying to you today? Look, we've got two kinds of people: one kind are people who refuse to let themselves feel anything at all; they sort of harden themselves and they say, "I'm not going to care. I'm not going to care. I don't care at all." That's one extreme. That's no great help. Now, the second kind I'm talking about are the people who are upset but, through understanding, transcend it. Get over it.

And as for Paul saying he does things that he doesn't want to do, etc., he does ask, who will get me out of this? The grace of Christ will get me out of it. Now, the grace of Christ comes through so many ways. You must not understand the grace of Christ as being some substance that is poured into you. When you come to a deeper understanding of reality, is that not the grace of Christ? When you understand yourself better, is that not the grace of Christ? So there it is.

~ *You've been programmed with certain values all your life, and in your relationships you're*

called to compromise some of those values. Even
though you understand that other people have
also been programmed, where do you draw the
line and how much do you compromise—or
do you just quit? Also, if you understand that
your programming upsets you, how do you
free yourself from being upset when you are
overwhelmed with problems that are beyond your
control?

Be patient. Don't expect to do all of this in twenty-four hours. Some people are lucky; they seem to see it in a flash, and it makes all the difference to them. Others take time. They take weeks, they take months. But I can assure you of this: Get started, and you'll see the results within a week. The upsets will still keep coming, depending on the depth of the programming.

Now, about the second part of your question. One doesn't have to compromise on any values, on what is good and bad. One doesn't compromise on that at all in dealing with others. One doesn't do evil to get the love of people, or to get their goodwill, or to get their approval.

I'm giving so much so quickly, in such a short time, that understandably it's going to be somewhat confusing. But as the time goes, particularly if you listen with an open mind, things will become clearer by themselves. Talk about an open mind: Did you hear about the guy from Brooklyn who was in the Sahara Desert in swimming trunks, for heaven's sake, and a towel? Walking in the Sahara Desert, he meets an Arab, and he says, "Hi." And the Arab says, "Hi." He asks, "How far away from here is the sea?"

"The sea? For heaven's sake," says the Arab, "that's a thousand miles away from here." And the guy from Brooklyn says, "Boy, some beach you guys have out here."

A beach?

Open mind, open mind.

Stories That Carry the Message

The Gift of Fire

There's this guy who invented fire. He takes the tools for making fire and goes up to the north, where there are some tribes shivering in the cold. He teaches them the art and the advantages of making fire. And the people become interested. They learn. And what do you know? Pretty soon they're cooking, they're using the fire for building And before they had time to say thanks to the inventor, he had disappeared. He didn't want any thanks; he just wanted people to benefit from his invention.

He goes to another tribe, and he attempts to interest them also in his new invention. But he ran into a snag there, see? The priests began to realize how popular the guy was becoming and how their own influence on the people was diminishing. So they decided to poison him. A suspicion arose among the people that it was the priests who had done it, so you know what the priests did?

They had a huge portrait made of the man. They put it on the main altar in the temple. They devised a liturgy by which the man would be honored, a ritual; and year after year, people came to pay homage to the great inventor and to the instruments for making fire. And the ritual was faithfully observed. But there was no fire. No fire. Ritual. Remembrance. Gratitude. Veneration. Yes. But no fire.

"Why do you call me Lord, Lord, and fail to do what I tell you?"

What's he telling us? Love. Love. That's what he's saying. What's the major obstacle to love? What I've been talking about today: Our programming.

Our obsessive attachments. Those are what's blocking it, as I hope to show you during this session. The best religion in the world is the religion called Love. Not the religion called Lord, Lord. Who says this thing about Love? Jesus Christ Himself. And may we never lose sight of that, we Christians.

Grace and Effort

Talking about this matter of grace and our effort, I think of the lovely story of the pious old man who said one day to God, "God, look how faithfully I've served you all my life, right?" Of course, he heard no answer.

"Right," said he to himself. "Now, I've never asked you for anything, right?"

"Right," said he, talking on behalf of God, of course. And he said, "Now, I'm going to ask you for just one favor and you can't say no to me. All my life I've served you, I've observed the law, I've kept the rites. I've done good to people, I've observed your commandments. Just do me this one favor: Let me win the lottery, and then I can retire in peace and security."

So he was convinced that God would grant him his desire, and he waited and waited and waited. And he kept on praying every night. And after six months, nothing had happened. And then one night, in sheer frustration, he yelled: "God, give me a break. Let me win the lottery."

And imagine the fright he got when he heard a voice reply, "Give me a break yourself. Buy a ticket."

He hadn't bought a ticket.

Make sure you get your ticket. Make sure you're using your understanding. Don't expect miracles to happen. See, understand, and change as a result of that.

The Wealth of the Sannyasi

The second point I want to make before we end has to do with happiness. I'm going to tell you one of my favorite stories. You know, sometimes a story says more than a whole day's lecture because it speaks to the depths within us, and this one certainly speaks to mine. This is a story of a guy who is moving out of his village in India, and he sees what we in India call a sannyasi. The sannyasi is the wandering mendicant. This is the person who, having attained enlightenment, understands that the whole world is his home and the sky is his roof, and God is his father and will look after him, so he moves from place to place the way you and I would move from one room of our home to another.

Here was this wandering sannyasi, and the villager, when he meets him, says, "I cannot believe this."

And the sannyasi says, "What is it you cannot believe?"

And the villager says, "I had a dream about you last night. I dreamt that the Lord Vishnu said to me, 'Tomorrow morning, you will leave the village around 11 o'clock, and you'll run into this wandering sannyasi.' And here, I've met you."

"What else did the Lord Vishnu say to you?" asks the sannyasi.

And the man replies, "He said to me, 'If the man gives you a precious stone he has, you will be the richest man in the whole world.' Would you give me the stone?"

So the sannyasi says, "Wait a minute." He rummages in his little knapsack that he had. He asks, "Would this be the stone you're talking about?" And the man couldn't believe his eyes because it was a diamond—the largest diamond in the world.

He holds the diamond in his hands and he asks, "Could I have this?"

And the sannyasi says, "Of course, you could take it. I found it in a forest. You're welcome to it." And he goes on, and sits under a tree on the outskirts of the village. The man grasps this diamond, and how great is his joy.

This is the way our joy feels, isn't it, the day we get something we really want? Do you ever stop to ask how long it lasts? You got the girl you wanted, right? You got the boy you wanted, right? You got that car, huh? You got the degree. You were first in your university class. How long does the joy last? Let's measure it. I mean that. How many seconds? How many minutes? You get tired of it, don't you? Then you are looking for something else, aren't you?

Why don't we study this? It is more valuable than studying the scriptures—because what good is it to you to study the scriptures and crucify the Messiah on the basis of them, as Jesus was, if you've not understood this? If you've not understood what it means to live, and to be free, and to be spiritual?

So, the guy has the diamond. And then instead of going home, he sits under a tree, and all day he sits, immersed in thought. And toward evening, he goes to the tree where the sannyasi is sitting, gives him back the diamond, and says, "Could you do me a favor?" "What?" says the sannyasi.

"Could you give me the riches that make it possible for you to give this thing away so easily?"

Boy, I love that story. Could you give me the riches that make it possible for you to give this away so easily? That is what I've been talking about today.

The world is full of sorrow. The root of sorrow is attachment. The uprooting of sorrow is the dropping of attachment. The understanding that attachment is a false belief—the false belief that anything or any person can make you happy. True happiness is caused by nothing. True happiness is uncaused. If you ask the mystic why he or she is happy, the answer will be, "Why not?" No block, no obstruction. Why not?

Have you ever thought that if something causes your happiness, when you lose that something then your happiness will be destroyed? Has it ever occurred to you that if something causes your happiness you will become possessive of that thing? That you will become anxious lest you lose it? Whatever that thing be—learning, reputation, good health, life itself. Yet how interesting: the rediscovery of life. You will never live until you stop clinging to life. Let go. When you cling, happiness dies. If your happiness depends on anyone or anything, that's not happiness. That's anxiety. That's tension. That's pressure. That's fear.

How Sweet It Is

The Japanese have a powerful tale for this. Oh, it's so powerful. There's this guy who's running away from a tiger. He comes to a precipice. And quite unwittingly, he begins to slide down that precipice. And as he's sliding, he grabs hold of the branch of a tree that's growing there, a kind of bush. Then he looks down. There's no way of climbing up, and anyway, there's the tiger waiting for him at the top. If he slides down, he slides down to his death, 15,000 feet. What does he do? He has only a few minutes to live.

He looks at that bush he's holding onto and he finds it's a berry bush. He's holding onto it with one hand, and he plucks a berry with the other, puts it into his mouth, and tastes it. And as the story goes, "It tasted so sweet." Isn't that marvelous?

I know friends of mine in the past—two of them at different intervals—who were dying, and who said to me, "I began to truly taste life and see how sweet it was when I let go. I realized that life was ending. It was then that it began to taste sweet." So, paradoxically, we're doing all the wrong things to be happy.

We've been programmed to be unhappy. Anything we're doing to be happy is going to make us more unhappy. What are you going to do? Are you going to change yourself? Are you going to change others? Are you going to acquire something? You don't have to do anything. You have to understand. Drop the obstruction. Drop the false belief. The attachment will drop, and then you'll know what happiness is.

So easily said. If you would meditate on that for days, and you would experience some of its truth, then you won't need to listen to me or to anyone else. You will have it. You will have learned it. You will have seen it. You're attached now only because you falsely believe that without this thing or that person or situation or event, you will not be happy. You falsely believe that. See its falseness, and you will be free. How simple.

And here we are, scouring the earth, running everywhere in search of happiness. Yet we had it right here at home and did not understand it. And we listened to all kinds of sermons, and we studied all kinds of books, and we went to all kinds of churches—but we never heard it. We never recognized the Messiah, even though he was right there. Happiness was right there staring at us, right under our nose. We didn't see it.

Troubles with Human Relationships?

You're having trouble with people? You find some-body selfish, moody, unreliable, rejecting, stupid, intolerable, irresponsible—you name it. Think of the troubles you have with human relations. Do you know the root of all of those problems? Hold onto your chairs. You. They? No, you, you. You're having trouble? You're the cause. How come you're affected?

You come to me and you say, "Doctor, I've got stomach cramps. It's awful. It really is awful."

Then I, as your doctor, say, "You know, I'll pre-scribe something for your wife."

And you're saying, "Okay, that already makes me feel better, Doctor. Thanks."

Now, isn't that crazy? Who's having the trouble? You, right? But we've been brought up to think that everybody else has to change.

If you're upset, there's something wrong with you. Let's clean that up first. You say, "But you mean she's not wrong?" She is wrong. "You mean, she shouldn't change?" Of course, she should. But you're not the guy who's going to change her, you know. Because you need to change first.

How about taking the beam out of your eye? Then you could take the speck out of hers.

You're not even seeing her. You know why? Because when you're upset, your telescope is out of focus. When you're upset, your window is blurred. And fool that you are, you're going now to straighten out all the buildings because your window is blurred with the rain. Could we clean your window first? That's what I'm attempting to do for you: clean the window through which you view others. Then you'll know what needs to be done and what doesn't need to be done.

We see people not as they are but as we are. And it's amazing how in the beginning we saw people as rude; then when we change, we see frightened people. They're so scared, poor things, that they're driven to hostility. Then you're understanding, you're compassionate, whereas before, you'd react with anger, with hate. "Hey, wait a minute. Why is he being rude?" You're too upset to see. You're too upset to realize. Could we clean you up first? Oh, no, no; you've come to me so that I can prescribe medicine for everyone else.

We're all in the change business, aren't we? We want to change ourselves, we want to change the world. That's what our stupid programming has done to us. What you need is not change, but understanding. Understand yourself. Understand others.

I'm going to say something that's perfectly scandalous, but it's true: You're not here to change the world. You're here to love the world. And, by damn, you don't want to love the world, you want to change it. You know what it means to love? To love is to see. To see. How can you love what you don't even see? And how can you see when there's any strong emotion—here comes another shock—positive or negative, coming in the way?

They say that love is blind. Rubbish. There's nothing so clear-sighted as love. It's the most clear-sighted thing in the world. It's attachment that is blind. Because it's stupid. Because it's based on a false belief. And they call that love? "I'm in love with you. I love you." What? You love me, or you love yourself? You know what *in love* means? *In love* means: "I want you for me." *In love, I am in love,* means "I'm possessive of you." *To be in love with you* means "I want you for me; I'm not going to be happy without you; I emotionally depend on you; I can't be happy without you."

That's a drug. That's a disease. Your culture and mine tells us that it's the supreme virtue. That's garbage, but who dares to say this? You're blind. You're full of yourself when you're in love. Ever thought of that? You don't see the other person; you've projected a hopeful image onto that person and that's what you're loving. Hopeful. When we're not expecting anything from the other person, we don't say we're in love.

So if you're having trouble relating to others, take a look at yourself. Ask yourself why you are upset. Where is it coming from? It's from your programming, that's where. I've sometimes been amazed that people who would irritate me by their behavior don't seem to irritate others. I ask, "How come he doesn't get annoyed when exposed to this behavior? How come I do? There's something wrong with me." And here I was, busy trying to change that irritating person. Now, when I'm not upset, oh, then that's fine. Then I might suggest things, I might do things. I'm qualified to enter into the change, into any activity involving change. But not until then. My telescope is out of focus.

Oh, here's a great secret for improving human relations. How much it has helped me! Any time I'm having trouble with anyone, if I'm upset, I have this talk with myself: "Hey, Tony, there's something wrong with you. How about you and I sit down and take a good look at this, okay?"

"Okay. But I'm still dying to say . . . "

"No, no, you're upset. This isn't coming from

him, it isn't coming from you; it's coming from your programming." Oh, well, I see. All of a sudden, there's perspective. There's distance. There's understanding. There's love, at last. And oh, that can be quite hard to achieve. You can be quite hard, love can be quite hard, but love is fair. Love is just. Love sees. Love is not prejudiced. Okay, so much for human relations.

Love Is No Bargain

A big lie that we were told when we were kids is the following: You need to be loved. When you're a kid, yes, granted, that's okay. Let's not quarrel about that. But what if you're sixty-four years old? You're twenty-five years old? You're eighteen? You know what they're still telling you? You need to be loved. You need to be a success. You need to be approved. You need to be appreciated. You need to be affirmed. You need . . . rubbish. And everybody's believing this.

I'll tell you what you need. There's only one need. This comes from many years of reflection. There's only one need, there's only one emotional need, and that is *to* love. *To love.* No other need.

"You mean, I don't need *to be* loved?"

Wait a minute. May I know what you're talking about when you say, "to be loved"? Are you talking about a need to be desired? Is that what you're talking about—your need to be desired? That is what everybody's talking about—in other words, "No one seems to desire me." You want to be desired? And you want all the consequences of that desire, with all the control and the manipulation? Is that what you're talking about?

You need to be appreciated. Good. Watch this one; I'm going to dramatize it for you. Once you begin to understand yourself, you begin to understand other people, and sometimes that's amusing. You're thinking, *Here comes old so-and-so; watch how I'm going to make him happy, okay?* Or, you say, "Hey, Tom, you look great this morning. My God, you look twenty years younger." Whoosh. Tom's so happy. Or, "That was a great sermon you gave, you know?" He's thrilled. You could twirl them around your little finger.

Maybe you've done that. You can do anything with these human monkeys. Just tell them you like them, and tell them something good about themselves. First, they're thrilled; second, they'll love you. What they call love, of course, is monkey love.

You know what that love is? Watch. "You be good to me, I'll be good to you, okay? You give me what I want, I'll like you, okay? You don't give me what I want, I'll dislike you, okay?"

This is supposed to be love?

This is what I call a good bargain. You find this "love" in the marketplace, on Wall Street. It's supposed to be love, but nobody's telling us this. Nobody's analyzing this for us—or at least very few. I never heard anybody say, "Hey, what you're calling love is really a bargain. It's an exchange. It's a barter. It's a business deal." I've been reading books on marriage written by all kinds of religious people. They don't seem to have the slightest notion of this.

Basically, it's "You be nice to me, I'll be nice to you. You're not nice to me, you betray me, you're disloyal to me, you're unfaithful to me, and naturally I'm angry with you and I'm upset." And everybody's saying, "Right, naturally." Naturally? You call that love? So, here comes the computer. Press the red button and you praise him; Woo, he's so happy. Press the blue button, and criticize him; Bang, he's on the floor. You like to be that way?

We've got books on psychology, written by the most prestigious psychologists in the world, telling us that that's the way to be. When people tell you you're okay, naturally you're supposed to feel great. And when they tell you you're not okay, naturally you're supposed to feel down. This is supposed to be human. I call it being a machine.

I read a story the other day of a woman who said to her teenage son, "What does Mary see in you? What does she like in you?"

He replied, "What Mary likes in me is, A, that I'm handsome; B, that I'm intelligent; and C, that I'm great company."

And his mother asked, "What do you like in Mary?"

He replied, "What I like in Mary is that she finds me, A, intelligent; B, handsome . . ."

They're so stupid, believe me. If you just tell them you like them, they'll like you. That's how stupid people are. These are computers, machines with mechanical reactions. "Why don't you buy your newspaper somewhere else? Look how rude he is." "Why should he decide where I buy my newspaper? Why should his behavior decide what I do with my life?" Isn't that beautiful?

But as for you, you must be like your heavenly Father—all-loving and all-compassionate. For He makes His sun to shine on good and bad alike.

Makes His rain to fall on saints and sinners alike. What do you know? If you only greet those who greet you, you're a monkey like the rest. You're a computer and are being mechanical. How come we didn't find it out? It was staring us in the face and we hadn't seen it.

We've Been Drugged

Take a little child, six months old, and inject heroin, or any other drug, into the body of this child. And suppose you keep injecting the drug into this child; after a while, the whole body of the child is craving the drug. Craving desperately for the drug. See, it hasn't been brought up on good, healthy nutrition; the child's been brought up on the drug. And so when you deprive the child of the drug, the poor thing goes through the agonies of death, in the body of the child.

Ready for a surprise? That's what happened to you and me—to all of us. They drugged us when we were kids. They didn't bring us up on the healthy, wholesome nourishment of play and work and beauty and the pleasures of the senses, and as we grew older, the pleasures of the mind. Oh, no.

They gave us a taste for a drug called "approval." A drug called "success." A drug called "making it to the top, achieving." Affirmation. Triumph. Victory. They gave us power, reputation, fame, prestige. They gave us the drugs.

And you know something? We began to feel good. It was a giddy feeling when they were applauding us. We started thinking how it was great to be famous, how great to be successful, how great to be popular. But as we began to grow, they could control us in any way they liked. All they had to do was withhold the drug.

Boy, if you haven't gone through this, I salute you. They don't approve of you? How uneasy you feel, how restless. They criticize you? They're not affirming you? Withdrawal symptoms—you're crawling back for reassurance. And the psychologists are writing books telling you this is the way to be, this is the way to be. More of the drug. More control.

Now, as a result of this drug, you've lost your ability to love. Because when you *need* someone, you cannot love that person. Do you know why? Because you can't see that person anymore. When a politician needs the votes, he stops seeing the people. When business people become crazy over profits, they stop seeing people. When I want something from you, I'm not seeing you—I want to get something out of you.

And do you know, it's so bad that twenty-four hours of the day, consciously or unconsciously, we want something from the people around us. We want their approval. We dread their disapproval; we're scared they'll reject us; we're scared what they will think of us. How could you love people like this when you're so dependent on them emotionally?

Oh, we've got to depend on one another, they'll tell you grandly. Of course, we've got to depend on one another. That's how society grows. We share the labor, we share our caring. That's marvelous; I have nothing against that kind of dependence. The evil is where you depend on another for your happiness. To depend on another for learning, for technical skills, for food—that's fine. For more co-operation in the world, that's wonderful. But to depend on another for your happiness, that's evil. Now, you cannot love. Give it a thought later, when you have time and leisure.

Once you stop depending on others, when you extinguish the need for other people—when you first get in touch with this—it's terrifying because you suddenly become alone. Not lonely, but alone.

It's a strange feeling. You suddenly understand what you've been all along, but you had not seen it. And you suddenly realize how lovely it is to be alone, how nice not to need others emotionally. And for the first time you understand that you can love people.

You no longer need to bribe people, you don't need to manipulate them, you don't need to impress them. You don't need to placate them. At last, you can love. And for the first time in your life, you are incapable of loneliness. You cannot be lonely anymore. You know what "loneliness" means? It's a desperate need for people, to the point that you're unhappy without people. Loneliness is not cured by human company. Loneliness is cured by contact with reality—by understanding that you don't need people. At last you can enjoy other people because you don't need them.

There's no tension anymore. Do you know what it means to be with people and to have no tension? Because you don't give a damn whether they like you or not, don't care what they think of you. Do you know what that means? Freedom. Joy. They can think what they want, they can say what they want. That's all right. You're not affected. You've gotten the drug out of your system.

And oh, yes, you're still in the world; you're just no longer of it. They can't control you anymore. And all of a sudden, you have nowhere to rest your head. The foxes have their holes, the birds have their nests. But you're not resting your head anywhere because you don't need to. Because you don't cling anymore. That's when love begins.

Parable of the Tourists on the Bus

Well, I've given you so much to meditate on. Guess I got carried away. I'll offer a little parable and then we'll end with a story that, if I had to choose one of the thousands of stories I know, I would call my favorite story.

The parable: A group of tourists is sitting in a bus. They're passing through the most gorgeous countryside. The drapes are drawn in the bus, so nobody sees a thing. And what do you think the people inside are doing? They're fast asleep, some of them, and others are quarreling about who's the best-dressed woman on the bus. Who's the guy who's sitting in best seat on the bus? And so it goes on to the journey's end. None of them has seen anything of this gorgeous countryside.

What do you think most people are spending their lives doing? Impressing others, that's what. Making sure they're not criticized. Getting affirmation. I wonder how many human beings there are who are not obsessed with this, twenty-four hours of the day, consciously or not. Very few, I venture. The consequence? Very few people actually live. You'll never rediscover life until you understand this falsehood, which our culture, our society—and, I'm sorry to say, to some extent even many of the world religions—are perpetrating. They are the enemies of life.

The Lion Who Thought He Was a Sheep

And here's the story: There was a lion that grew up in a flock of sheep and so he had no consciousness that he was a lion. He didn't know he was a lion. He would bleat like a sheep, he'd eat grass like a sheep. One day they were wandering at the edge of a big jungle when a mighty lion let out a big roar and leaped out of the forest and right into the middle of the flock. All the sheep scattered and ran away. Imagine the surprise of the jungle lion when he saw this other lion there among the sheep. So, he gave chase. He got hold of him. And there was this lion, cringing in front of the king of the jungle. And the jungle lion said to him, "What are you doing here?"

And the other lion said, "Have mercy on me. Don't eat me. Have mercy on me." But the king of the forest dragged him away, saying "Come on with me." And he took him to a lake and he said, "Look." So, the lion who thought he was a sheep looked, and for the first time he saw his reflection. He saw his image. Then he looked at the jungle lion, and he looked in the water again, and he let out a mighty roar. He was never a sheep again. It took only one minute.

• • •

Well, maybe in the course of all my talking one of you will have looked carefully and seen through this network of lies and conditionings and programmings that we've all been subjected to. Maybe you have some inkling now into who you are. Then, these words will have been worthwhile.